LOUISIANAeats!

LOUISIANAeats!

The People, the Food, and Their Stories

Written by Poppy Tooker • Photographs by David G. Spielman

PELICAN PUBLISHING COMPANY
GRETNA 2013

The word "Pelican" and the depiction of a pelican are trademarks of Pelican Publishing Company, Inc., and are registered in the U.S. Patent and Trademark Office.

Library of Congress Cataloging-in-Publication Data

Tooker, Poppy.
  Louisiana eats! : the people, the food, and their stories / by Poppy Tooker ; photography by David G. Spielman.
      pages cm
  Includes index.
  ISBN 978-1-4556-1876-7 (hardcover : alk. paper) — ISBN 978-1-4556-1877-4 (e-book) 1. Cooking, American—Louisiana style. 2. Cooks—Louisiana—Interviews. 3. Louisiana—Social life and customs. I. Spielman, David G., 1950 photographer. II. Title.
  TX715.2.L68T64 2013
  641.59763—dc23
                                                                        2013022322

Printed in the United States of America
Published by Pelican Publishing Company, Inc.
1000 Burmaster Street, Gretna, Louisiana 70053

Contents

Preface

On a beautiful, bright spring Tuesday in 2009, the smiling, blonde powerhouse Diana Pinckley walked up to me at the Crescent City Farmers Market and asked, "What would you think about doing a radio show?" "I think I could do that," I responded, and that is how my WWNO FM public radio show, *Louisiana Eats!,* came to be.

That was the typical sort of magic that Pinckley, as her friends all called her, knew how to conjure. I had seen her brilliant, creative mind at work, dreaming up ways to brand and promote projects on which we worked together such as the Crescent City Farmers Market and Edible Schoolyard New Orleans.

The biggest challenge in getting the new WWNO food show started was naming it. The sponsors had been lined up, the first airdate scheduled, and we were all still ruminating on it. That problem resolved in the Contemporary Crafts tents at Jazz Fest when Pinckley's husband, John Pope, suggested we call it "Louisiana Eats!"

Consequently, the radio show you hear today might never have existed without the "Pinkalopes," as John and Diana's friends refer to them. Tragically, we lost Diana in a courageous battle with cancer in September 2012, and she is sorely missed in every corner of New Orleans.

Louisiana Eats! has given me the opportunity to speak with people I never even imagined meeting—never mind having an in-depth conversation with them. Anthony Bourdain, Harold McGee, David Chang, Jeff Corwin, Andrew Zimmern, and countless local food celebrities have all shared lively banter with me on the show.

In the first season of the show in 2011, we spoke with every one of the celebrity chefs on Bravo TV's *Top Chef Masters*. With incredible luck, our interviews rolled out in the identical order of the popular show's eliminations. Our last interview was taped and aired just before Floyd Cardoz was named that season's Top Chef Master.

I've learned so much along the way and am privileged to have captured some amazing oral histories that I suspect will age well with time. To me, that has been the greatest gift of *Louisiana Eats!* With the help of Thomas Walsh, my co-producer and sound engineer, I have maintained a meticulous catalog of raw, unedited audio recordings from *Louisiana Eats!* interviews. All of the shows are archived on the WWNO Web site.

In writing this book, I've transcribed the guests' actual spoken words, some of which I pulled from previously unaired audio. That process frequently took me back into the moment, allowing me to share my personal observations and memories that surround the people of *Louisiana Eats!*, most of whom I regard as dear friends.

We've spent time in the city with Leah Chase, who let Thomas record our conversation as we drove to New Orleans' Gallier Hall for the kick-off of the 2012 Carnival season. Once there, the whole city helped celebrate Leah's eighty-ninth birthday, complete with a "Happy Birthday" serenade from New Orleans mayor Mitch Landrieu. We've also gone into the swamps with alligator hunter Joey Fonseca and spent time at Louisiana's farmers markets, recording hours of interviews.

More than a decade before *Louisiana Eats!* began airing, my involvement with the New Orleans culinary community began when I founded Slow Food New Orleans, one of the first local chapters established in the US. For those who may have little working knowledge of Slow Food, I offer the following: Slow Food is an international organization founded in 1986 by visionary Italian leader Carlo Petrini. Prompted by the opening of a McDonald's at the Spanish Steps in Rome, Carlo and his food-activist friends began a movement that is active in more than eighty countries.

Originally, Carlo set out to combat the effects of fast food in our lives. Now, his work encompasses and has influenced everything from farmers markets to school lunch programs, from the artisan food world to that of food crafters of all kinds, working to provide a better-laid table for us all.

In the very early days of Slow Food in the US, Carlo traveled to New Orleans to promote his relatively new concept, the Salone del Gusto. The Salone is an international showcase of the world's finest food and drink held bi-annually in Turin, Italy. During Carlo's visit—his first to New Orleans—we lunched at Uglesich's, sitting next to sacks of potatoes, and he rang the opening bell at the Saturday Crescent City Farmers Market. Carlo wept at the taste of the snowball prepared for him by Ernest and Mary Hansen of Hansen's Sno-Bliz, a New Orleans original since 1939.

As you read *Louisiana Eats!*, again and again you will read about Slow Food's "Ark of Taste." The Ark is a virtual Noah's Ark, wherein endangered foods of the world are protected. Carlo presented his brilliant Ark concept in 1996 in Turin, Italy, at the premiere Salone del Gusto. After working for years to promote and preserve New Orleans' cultural food treasures such as the calas, I loved the Ark concept and turned into a Slow Food diehard. I became an international governor with the movement and traveled to meetings in Santorini, Greece, and Oporto, Portugal.

Along with people who became beloved colleagues and friends, such as the author Deborah Madison, I served on the original Slow Food USA Ark of Taste committee and later became the committee chair. During that time, with the help of local partners such as the Crescent City Farmers Market's founder and executive director, Richard McCarthy, Slow Food New Orleans used Carlo's brilliant Ark concept to help save vital, cultural Louisiana foods such as Creole cream cheese. It's no small coincidence that our very own homegrown Richard McCarthy is the executive director of Slow Food USA today, or that much of *Louisiana Eats!* comes with a serving of Slow Food on the side.

This book is not primarily a cookbook, although each chapter includes at least one recipe pertinent to the storyline. Many of them are mine or my great-grandmother's, though some were generously given to me by cooking icons such as Leah Chase and Joan Nathan. I promise you, each one is delicious.

David Spielman's portraits are intended as food for thought. Each of the fifteen people portrayed in these pages is someone very special who, if you don't know by now, you should get to know if you have the chance!

I hope that *Louisiana Eats!* will find a place in your home and that you will enjoy visiting it with me time and time again.

Poppy Tooker
New Orleans, Louisiana

LOUISIANA eats!

Red Beans and Rice—Sure Is Nice!

Monday in New Orleans means red beans and rice. This simple dish has been part of the rhythm of life in New Orleans since the city's earliest days, a tradition thought to have arrived with the first French settlers. Mondays were wash day, and red beans were the perfect thing to cook, utilizing the hambone from Sunday dinner. This was a single-pot meal that was best if simmered all day while the laundry chores were done. Creole chef Leah Chase says that New Orleans red beans were not meant for other days of the week and complains (in a joking fashion) that until tourists demanded them all week long, they were a Monday-only special at her restaurant, Dooky Chase's.

One fine spring Tuesday, as I shopped at the Crescent City Farmers Market in uptown New Orleans, I paused for a visit with one of my favorite farmers, Nick Usner. Nick is part of the wave of young farmers beginning to show up at market, and his offerings often include exquisite baby beets and other unusual, often heirloom, varieties of vegetables, fragrant herbs, and tiny cartons of quail eggs.

That day, his selection included baggies of something that looked like red beans—but they were neither dry nor cooked. "And what it this?" I asked. "Poppy," Nick laughed, "they're red beans!"

"Fresh red beans?" I replied, and Nick nodded. "But how do you cook them?" He really laughed then. "You cook them just like you cook the dried ones—except these cook quicker and are just creamier and tastier than any dried bean I've ever cooked," he said.

Nick explained, "They're a cool-weather crop, so they can be grown in the spring and the fall here. I harvest them before they dry, because my goal is to sell them fresh while they are at their peak flavor and peak nutritional value." Sometimes, he shells the red beans and freezes them fresh. "You can completely skip the soaking process, so you save a little cooking time as well."

Nick's father was an organic pig farmer in Bush, Louisiana, who died young but left Nick with a love of the land and an understanding of the importance of good stewardship. Nick told me, "I think a lot about my path at Grow Farm and how, if it hadn't been for my dad stressing the importance of organics and taking care of the environment and the soil, which we pull our livelihood from, I probably wouldn't be an organic farmer today."

Nick was one of the first market farmers to gain organic certification. His one-acre farm is a laboratory of sorts, where he experiments with new varieties and new growing methods of produce.

But fresh red beans? I asked everyone I knew if they'd ever seen or cooked with fresh red beans. Universally, the answer was, "No." I'd never thought of it before, and it seemed that the entire culinary community of the Crescent City believed that the Monday staple needed drying and an all-day simmer.

Nick informed me that fresh red beans were commonplace in the little town of Bush. He invited me to come visit his Northshore farm, promising to introduce me to a neighboring farmer, Homer Dutch, whose family had been growing red beans for generations.

Taking Nick up on his offer, I drove across the twenty-four-mile Causeway across Lake Pontchartrain and followed shady country roads lined with tall pines to find Nick's farm. This was the first field recording I had ever done—in more than one sense of the word—and I had just begun working with a sound engineer who was a young, female transplant to the city.

She was redheaded and very fair, and on that very hot day, she arrived at Nick's farm wearing long sleeves and a veiled hat that at first glance looked like a beekeeper's garb. I couldn't resist asking if she wasn't unbearably hot in that getup. She assured me that she was fine, and we went on to tour Nick's farm, tasting the tiny shoots of asparagus that were just coming up and marveling at his astonishing varieties of figs.

At one point as we stood in his bean patch, I began to understand the young woman's clothing choice—although not necessarily cool, certainly effective. "The honey bees I have here help to perpetuate the beans," Nick pointed out. "I've noticed honey bees here in the beans all morning, and I also have noticed that having pollinators on the farm helps increase my yield. Every spring, at least sixty percent of the field is filled with legumes to both fixate nitrogen and give the pollinators a little nectar early on in the season. That also adds a lot of biomass back into the soil. The plants are tilled back into the soil at the end of the growing season."

Nick never stopped moving during our interview on the farm, as he was getting ready for market the next day. While we talked, he bunched yard-long beans, sometimes called asparagus beans, "even though they don't taste like asparagus," Nick remarked. "After red beans, we shift into growing edamame and yard-long beans, our summertime legumes," he explained.

The sound engineer and I traveled by separate cars down the road to nearby Waldheim, Louisiana. Homer Dutch and his friendly farm dogs met us at the gate, welcoming us in. Homer Dutch proudly gestured around his well-kept farm. "In German, 'Waldheim' means 'home in the woods.' My great-grandfather came from Germany in the mid-1800s and homesteaded here on this same property. My daddy was born here in 1903, and we've always grown fresh red beans!" he exclaimed. "They're so easy to produce, you just plant them, hope for rain, and try to keep the grass out. When the pods turn yellow, they're ready to pick."

Homer Dutch confirmed that his family seasons their fresh red beans on the Northshore just as we do our dried beans on the Southshore—with onions, garlic, and lots of pork. "Where do you get the seed for the red beans that you grow?" I asked. "Well," Mr. Dutch said, "I'm not sure how those Camellia people would feel about this, but we just go to the grocery and buy a one-pound package of red beans and plant them!"

Previously for *Louisiana Eats!,* I had interviewed Connelly Hayward, the fourth-generation owner of L. H. Hayward and Company, producer of Camellia Brand® beans. Once in the studio, Connelly shared the story of his family's business with me.

He began with a brief history of red beans in southern Louisiana, dating them back several hundred years, stating that "when the cane-field workers came here from Haiti, Jamaica, and parts of Cuba, they brought their native dish, red beans and rice. The way they would cook red beans was to put a pot on the fire and cook it down all day with all kinds of meat and seasonings and get this thick, stew-like consistency that we still enjoy today."

Lucius Hamilton Hayward, Connelly's great-grandfather, had founded the Camellia Bean Company in 1923. He was a general produce supplier at New Orleans' French Market. His son, William Gordon Hayward, followed him into the business. Business boomed for L. H. Hayward and Company during World War II. They received a contract to supply the US Army with beans.

After the war, William realized that supermarkets popping up everywhere were the wave of the future. Previously, customers bought their beans by scooping them from a barrel into a paper bag. The new supermarket customer wanted to pluck prepackaged bags from a shelf, place them in the basket, and roll up to the checkout counter.

Connelly's grandfather began to package beans for supermarkets, naming the new business Camellia after his wife's favorite flower. At the same time, William

became increasingly picky with the quality of his beans, demanding that his growers provide him with red kidney beans of a size and quality that exceeded USDA Grade A. Connelly said, "My grandfather chose where the beans would be grown. While they were growing, he would get samples from the field to examine and was also very hands-on in the field process of combining—picking up the beans. He dictated to the operators of the big co-op elevators how he expected his beans to be cleaned.

Connelly claims that Camellia is the only packager that cleans the beans again on-site before they are packaged in order to maintain the company's age-old quality of excellence. "So, that means, when they're clean, we clean them again," he said.

William Hayward's focus on quality and consistency resulted in a new grade of bean that is still recognized by all US dried-bean growers today. We now have a USDA Grade 2 bean, USDA Grade 1 bean, and the "Hayward" grade, the finest bean of all—proof that Camellia red beans really are a superior product. The superior grade, coupled with their popularity, ensures a rapid turnover on the supermarket shelf, resulting in a fresher dried bean for the consumer. This confirmed for me that it isn't just New Orleans culinary lore—or our communal food memory—that caused New Orleanians to favor Camellia beans.

I asked Connelly how he likes his red beans best. "When I was a child, Mother used to cook them with ham hock, bay leaf, a little bit of cumin, a little bit of thyme, and of course she'd put some onion and garlic in there and just let them simmer all day. I would come home from school and the whole house would smell so good," he answered.

Another story that Connelly shared with me during our interview was his tale of the Zulu coconut. "No written documentation exists," he said, "But my grandfather used to tell a story about wanting to diversify his business. So, he bought a container of coconuts, thinking it would be a great product. After they sat around for months, he could see that their shelf life was not going to last much longer.

"He asked and asked people about how to liquidate the stock and was about ready to pay someone to take them off of his hands. Some of his people who worked for him heard he was looking to get rid of the coconuts. These same employees marched in the Zulu organization and knew the Zulus were looking for anything to throw. So my grandfather made a deal with them, and the next thing you know, coconuts are flying off of floats!"

I asked Connelly whether his grandfather ever thought that coconut would become the iconic prize that it is today. "I don't think in his wildest imagination could he ever think it could have gotten to this," he answered. "I remember when I was a kid, he'd have some around the house and he'd give some to friends. But never—he could have never imagined. That's what you come to Mardi Gras for—to get a Zulu coconut!"

The official Zulu Web site dates the coconut throw back to 1910, when they were thrown in their natural "hairy" condition—a stark contrast with today's elaborately gilded and decorated version. Still, that sure is a fabulous family legend that the Haywards have told and retold over generations.

After meeting Homer Dutch in Waldheim, I called Connelly Hayward to share the news that Camellia red beans aren't just eaten weekly on Mondays but also annually planted as a crop! He found the news as fascinating as I did. Who would guess that New Orleans' favorite red beans doubles as seed for Louisiana farmers?

Fried Red Beans and Rice

Creamy red beans and rice are classic Louisiana eats, but they're showing up on restaurant menus in all sorts of new ways too. When a new restaurant, Capdeville, opened in the Central Business District of downtown New Orleans, I was amazed to see something on the menu they called "Fried Red Beans and Rice," a fresh take on a city standard that I'd never considered before. I quickly ordered some to see how it would compare with the classic dish.

I was served a basket of golden brown, golf-ball sized orbs with a savory dipping sauce on the side. Breaking them open, I was amazed to see red beans and rice, redolent with bits of smoked ham. The verdict? Delicious! Fried red beans and rice—it made me laugh out loud. You give it a try, and I'm sure you'll agree. This whimsical dish is a great new twist on a classic favorite.

Yields 1 dozen pieces

1 cup cooked rice
1 cup red beans, cooked creamy-style
4 green onions, thinly sliced
4 tbsp. finely chopped ham
2 tbsp. plus 1 cup dried breadcrumbs, divided

2 tsp. hot sauce
2 eggs, divided
½ cup milk
1 cup all-purpose flour
Oil for deep-frying

Mix together the rice, red beans, green onions, ham, and 2 tbsp. breadcrumbs. Sprinkle hot sauce over the mixture, and then stir in 1 egg to form a tight batter.

In another bowl, combine the milk and remaining 1 egg to make an egg wash.

Form small balls from the red beans and rice mixture, approximately the size of a golf ball. Roll in flour, then coat with the egg wash and roll in the remaining 1 cup breadcrumbs.

Heat the oil to 360 degrees and fry until golden brown. Drain on paper towels and serve immediately with Green Garlic Mayonnaise.

Green Garlic Mayonnaise

Yields 1 cup

1 clove garlic	Juice of 1 lemon
½ cup flat-leaf parsley, stems removed	1 cup olive oil
6 green onions	½ tsp. salt
1 egg	2 tbsp. ketchup

With a food processor running, drop in the garlic clove. Add the parsley and green onions and process until well chopped. Add egg and lemon juice. Slowly drizzle in olive oil. Add salt and ketchup. Continue processing until well mixed. Serve as a dipping sauce.

Roasted Okra

On the same *Louisiana Eats!* episode in which we visited with Nick Usner and Homer Dutch, I shared this recipe for roasted okra. Roasting okra completely eliminates the slime for which so many people claim to hate okra. Instead, during the roasting process, the mucilaginous nature of the okra is transformed into a silken mouthfeel. I've converted many an okra hater with this recipe!

Yields 6-8 servings

2 tbsp. olive oil
2 tbsp. balsamic vinegar
2 lbs. okra, the smaller, the better—if using larger pods, cut into 1" lengths

Salt to taste
Cayenne pepper or cumin to taste, if desired

Preheat the oven to 450 degrees. Lightly grease a baking pan.

Combine olive oil with balsamic vinegar in a large bowl. Add the okra to the bowl and toss until lightly coated. Arrange in a single layer on the baking pan.

Lightly sprinkle with salt, cayenne, or cumin, if desired.

Roast, stirring or shaking the pan every 5 minutes for about 10-15 minutes or until the okra is lightly browned. Serve hot or cold.

In the Kitchen with Leah

The Dooky Chase's Restaurant kitchen has been home to Leah Chase since she was just twenty-two. Even now, in her nineties, when a lifetime of standing on her feet has taken its physical toll, it's the place you're most likely to find her: standing at her stove, stirring a pot or making a roux. In the last couple of years, a folding table placed in the doorway of her two kitchens has served as a desk. She sits with her bad foot propped up on a milk crate, writing menus for the next day, barking orders like General Patton (one of her great heroes), and graciously receiving a countless stream of visitors who are looking to meet a legend.

When the federal levee system failed after Hurricane Katrina in 2005, four feet of water flooded Leah's restaurant as well as the homes of virtually every member of her family living in New Orleans. For almost four months, Baton Rouge became her temporary home. Leah and I had crossed paths in the culinary world many times before Hurricane Katrina, but, as with many of my friends and associates, I had no idea where the storm had stranded her.

In December 2005, our mutual friend Jessica Harris persuaded me to drive with her to Breaux Bridge for a lunch rendezvous with Leah and her daughters, Stella and Leah Jr. On that cold winter day, as we lingered over lunch, savoring every moment of normalcy, the future seemed bleak.

By January 2006, Leah and her husband, Edgar "Dooky" Chase II, had moved into a FEMA trailer just across the street from their famed Orleans Avenue restaurant, Dooky Chase's. There, I visited Leah, and we discussed the difficulties and intricacies of getting her back into her restaurant and kitchen.

Sometimes, I would persuade her to come out for lunch or dinner in one of the few places open in post-Katrina New Orleans. Over those meals, we forged a relationship that transcended the forty-plus-year age difference between us. Leah treated me like her contemporary, sharing the stories of great happiness and great grief that are her history.

A statement Leah made one day about the greatest loss

she'd ever suffered revealed exactly what that kitchen meant to her and how deeply Katrina's devastation had reopened that wound. Leah described experiencing the death of her forty-two-year-old daughter Emily, the one Leah described as her "cooking daughter," one of the only people who could ever step in for Leah in the kitchen.

"Emily died at one o'clock in the morning and I was in the kitchen that day by eleven," Leah said. The only way Leah could cope with the unthinkable loss of her daughter was through cooking—cooking for the countless friends and family members she knew would soon be at the restaurant's doors. She coped by honoring Emily, demonstrating that love in her kitchen.

Emily died unexpectedly due to complications during her eighth pregnancy, and her premature son, Nathan, lived for several months after his mother's death. Leah told me, "Little Nathan really saved us. With his mother gone, we had to focus on him, and it distracted us from the grief that was so terrible." After Nathan died, too, Leah still had her kitchen to console her. Hurricane Katrina had taken that away as well.

The restaurant had insurance, but mold remediation costs wiped that out quickly. Many generous people came together to bring Dooky Chase's Restaurant back. My husband, Nicky Mouledoux (an electrical engineer by trade but in reality a jack-of-all-trades), Jay Nix of Parkway Bakery, and Chef John Folse met again and again to strategize how it could be done and how much it would cost.

Painting, sheetrock, carpet, furnishings—pondering the many pieces needed to get Dooky Chase's open again was overwhelming. Chef John Folse, CEO of Chef John Folse and Company, reached out to his restaurant connections everywhere asking for help. John personally took on the task of redesigning and reequipping the kitchen. The original

Southbend stove that starred in Leah's reminiscences and that had fed everyone from Supreme Court justices to Michael Jackson had sat for weeks in Katrina's floodwaters. When Mr. Nestor Ibrahim, president of Southbend, offered to trade the original for a brand new range, the old Dooky Chase stove was shipped to Southbend, Indiana, where it is proudly displayed today in the company's museum.

Then, in the last week of November 2006, Nicky got bad news from the plumber. The old pipes under the kitchen's slab—all of the pipes, in fact—had broken apart "like they were in an earthquake." The plumber said they would have to be replaced.

With miraculous timing, one of our new New Orleanians, Ashley Graham, who was working on recovery efforts with the national nonprofit Share Our Strength, was assisting their for-profit partner, the Timberland Corporation, in planning the biggest volunteer day yet in post-Katrina New Orleans. Ashley cleverly arranged for all the top executives and board members from Timberland to volunteer for the day at Dooky Chase's. Jay Nix supervised one group as they floated and taped sheetrock. The others were sent to the kitchen to see Nicky, who had rented jackhammers to begin breaking up the slab.

When it was all over, we had put them through such intense physical labor that Ken Lombard Jr. begged, "Please, just tell us how much this is going to cost." At the time, Ken was vice president of entertainment for Starbucks. His employers quickly donated an unprecedented $180,000 to cover the repair costs. It was December 2006, and the happy news was like an early gift from Santa.

Triumphantly, in September 2007, Leah was able to reopen, first serving take-out only, and then, finally, welcoming guests into her beautifully refurbished dining rooms. The deep red walls were freshly painted and adorned with the work of the African-American artists whose work Leah had collected for many years. In fact, sometimes she had traded gumbo for art! Miraculously, Emily's son and one of Leah's grandsons, David Haydel, worked as a fireman at the time of Katrina, and he had been able to get into the restaurant and remove the artwork, saving it from the creeping mold.

On the fifth anniversary of Hurricane Katrina, Wednesday, August 29, 2010, *Louisiana Eats!* had been on the air for barely three months. While planning the editorial content, I realized the significance and impact of that potential *Louisiana Eats!* episode. As my personal post-Katrina story had been so interwoven with Leah's, she was the only interview I could imagine doing to commemorate the occasion.

Sound engineer Thomas Walsh had just begun working with me at that time. Not a native New Orleanian himself, Thomas had never met Leah or visited Dooky Chase's Restaurant. We met Leah after lunch service had wound down. She sat us in the Gold Room, originally a shotgun house where her in-laws, "Dooky" and Emily Chase, had first opened a sandwich shop in 1941.

With Thomas wielding the microphone, Leah and I began to recall the times we'd shared over the last five years. "It was terrible, really terrible. The water was two and half feet in here, five and a half feet in the bar. I had about fifty or sixty gallons of gumbo in the freezer and all the food in the refrigerator, so that was an awful mess that had to be cleaned out! We had no house. We had nothing! But FEMA gave us trailers and I appreciated FEMA for giving me that. I even liked the Red Cross meals—pork and beans and rice and a piece of bread. I was grateful for that!

"I didn't know where to go or what to do. When I came in here, for some reason I had no fear. I should have been afraid of everything but I wasn't and I just said, 'I know, I can get a broom and a mop and clean.' An electrician got the lights back on. Poppy, you know when we came in here, it was so terrible—it was awful. But people came from all over to help me clean up this thing."

With amazement, she continued. "I just cannot get over that! That's why I work so hard, because I feel like I gotta pay back! People do something for you and you have to pay them back some kind of way. Because people poured themselves in here. All these little ladies from Uptown came and cleaned chairs. People came from all over and offered me things to help me get back on my feet.

"I will forever be grateful. I have never seen that kind of outpouring in my life—never, never. Because here I am, I'm really not nobody, you know, really. But to see the vision these people had to know that, 'If I help to put this back, this will be one part of my city that can work and help to rebuild the rest of it.' I owe so many people, Poppy, I can't afford to die."

Thomas and I reconnected with Leah in April 2011 for an interview about the Creole tradition of eating gumbo z'herbes at Dooky Chase's on Holy Thursday. I asked her to describe the atmosphere in the restaurant each year on that day.

"You have the same people and they have their same table," Leah said. "They're ticky about their table. Mr. John Pope always has his table seven. Mr. Charbonnet always has his table nineteen. Everybody comes on that day. I don't care who you are in this city—you come. John Folse will come and sit in the middle of my dining room, all in his full chef's attire. So the people are passing by him at his table saying, 'Oh, Chef, that was very good,' and all he is saying is, 'Thank you,' and I'm the one in the kitchen, sweating it out!"

For listeners who never have tasted gumbo z'herbes, I asked Leah to explain this traditional and very superstitious dish that is so synonymous with her name. She said, "You have to use uneven numbers of greens—you can't have even numbers, that's bad luck. So get your greens, and you have either five, seven, nine, or eleven kinds of greens. Creoles believe that for each green in your Holy Thursday gumbo z'herbes, you'll make a new friend—and I always hope at least one of them will be rich!

"You have to wash those greens and boil them and grind them to make gumbo z'herbes. New Orleans has always been predominantly Catholic and that was the last meat day for Catholics before the Good Friday fast, so you put all kinds of meat in the gumbo z'herbes. You put stew meat, sausage, ham, chicken—all the works so you'd have a good hearty meal—and that was all you'd eat on Holy Thursday.

"We use collard, mustard, kale, cabbage, Swiss chard—I love to put beet tops in it. Creoles used to go on the neutral ground [referring to New Orleans' broad medians] and dig pepper grass and put that in. That gave it a little lemony flavor. Now that we can't find peppergrass I use watercress."

In late December 2011, I got a phone call from Mayor Mitch Landrieu's office asking if I could bring Leah to the annual Carnival Kickoff at Gallier Hall scheduled for Friday, January 6, 2012, Leah's eighty-ninth birthday. The mayor wanted to honor "Miss Leah" on her day in a special way.

Generously, Leah agreed to let Thomas be our "back-seat driver" to and from the celebration so that he could record our conversation for a *Louisiana Eats!* segment. When we picked Leah up, she reported that she'd been in the kitchen since six-thirty that morning.

When I asked what she'd been cooking, she said, "I do okra gumbo every Friday. I do lima beans and shrimp every Friday. So, today I made spaghetti and meatballs. I'm making eggplant farci so I cooked the eggplant."

Neither of us had ever attended the event before. We drove up to Gallier Hall and saw Zulu warriors in full Carnival costume along with political dignitaries and members of the Rex organization. Leah and I were seated on the front row, right next to New Orleans' first lady, Cheryl Landrieu.

Mayor Landrieu proclaimed to the audience, "I have a young lady here, who I am in love with . . ." Leah laughed out loud and responded, "You'd better mention your wife, darling." The mayor corrected his oversight and continued, "She watches over me. And anybody who knows her knows, if you get out of line, she's going to smack you around a little bit!

"The first time Obama dined at Dooky Chase—now this is the president of the greatest country in the free world I'm talking about—Miss Leah reprimanded him, saying, 'Mr. Obama, you do not put hot sauce in my gumbo before you even taste it!'" Then, Mayor Mitch sang "Happy Birthday" to Leah, and the whole city celebrated with king cake.

On the way home, Leah and I discussed the amazing news that our mutual friend, Dick Colton, had arranged for an exhibition of portraits of Leah at work in her kitchen painted by young Creole artist Gus Blache to be shown later that spring at the New Orleans Museum of Art. One of them was later added to the permanent collection of the National Art Gallery in Washington, DC.

In her usual self-depreciating way, Leah said, "It's all paintings of me in the kitchen of all places—me working and doing things in the kitchen. Poppy, I look like heck—my rear end looks like it's about five feet wide. But I don't care. It's me. I say, 'He painted me.' Although he could have made me look like Halle Berry or somebody, but he just made me look like me!"

What thrilled Leah most was the prospect that the exhibit might make people more interested in the arts, a part of life that Leah believes everyone should enjoy. In fact, the exhibit's gala opening raised more than a quarter-million dollars for an art endowment in Leah's honor dedicated to the acquisition of more African-American art at NOMA.

When the Gallier Hall event was over, I hurried Leah back to the kitchen because, for her eighty-ninth birthday, she had decided to open the restaurant for dinner for the first time since Hurricane Katrina. Not exactly what every eighty-nine-year-old woman would do to celebrate, but after all, Leah Chase is one of a kind.

Leah Chase's Gumbo z'Herbes

Here is Leah's special Holy Thursday Gumbo z'Herbes recipe, scaled down for your home kitchen.

Yields 10-12 servings

1 bunch mustard greens
1 bunch collard greens
1 bunch turnips
1 bunch watercress
1 bunch beet tops
1 bunch carrot tops
½ head lettuce
½ head cabbage
1 bunch spinach
2 medium onions, chopped
4 cloves garlic, chopped

Water
1 lb. smoked sausage
1 lb. smoked ham
1 lb. chaurice
1 lb. boneless brisket
5 tbsp. oil
¼ cup flour
1 tsp. thyme
1 tbsp. salt
1 tsp. cayenne pepper
3 tbsp. filé powder

Clean all greens thoroughly and coarsely chop. Place in a 12-quart stockpot with onions and garlic. Cover vegetables with water. Boil together for 30 minutes.

While greens cook, cut all meats into bite-sized pieces. Heat oil in a heavy skillet and brown all meats in batches; set aside. Add the flour to the oil and meat drippings in the pan and cook until flour is lightly browned.

Drain the vegetables and reserve all cooking liquid. Add browned meats and roux to the stockpot.

In a food processor, purée all greens together. Add to the stockpot with thyme, salt, and cayenne pepper. Add 2 quarts of the reserved liquid. Bring to a boil, reduce to a simmer, and cook for at least 40 minutes. Adjust seasonings as needed. Remove from heat and whisk in the filé powder. Serve at once over rice.

Leah's Crab Soup

I'll never forget the first time I saw Leah make this soup. She dumped a bushel of live crabs in the deep kitchen sink and began breaking them apart with her bare hands—something I'd never attempt! I'm much too afraid of those snapping claws.

Yields 6 servings

3 medium blue crabs
½ cup vegetable oil
3 tbsp. all-purpose flour
¾ cup chopped onions
½ cup chopped celery
½ cup chopped green pepper
1½ qts. water

1 clove chopped garlic
1 tsp. thyme
½ tsp. cayenne pepper
1 tsp. paprika
1 tbsp. chopped parsley
2 tsp. salt
½ lb. white crab meat

Clean crabs and cut into halves.

Heat oil in a pot. Add crabs; fry in hot oil for 10 minutes. Lower heat. Remove crabs; set aside.

To the remaining oil, add the flour, stirring constantly. Cook until light brown. Add onions and celery and cook until the onions are translucent. Add the green pepper and cook for about 3 to 4 minutes. Add water, pouring slowly while stirring. Add garlic, thyme, cayenne pepper, paprika, parsley, and salt. Return crabs to pot; let cook for 30 to 40 minutes.

Stir in white crab meat and simmer for 5 minutes.

Chicken and Shrimp Clemenceau

The classic French dish Clemenceau is usually prepared in New Orleans using either chicken or shrimp. Leah and I combined the two for a special cooking demonstration we did together at the Crescent City Farmers Market on the first Saturday that the downtown market reopened after Hurricane Katrina.

Yields 6 servings

2 cups peeled and diced Idaho potatoes (about 2 medium potatoes)
Oil for frying
3 boneless chicken breasts
¾ cup butter, divided, plus additional as needed
1 cup mushrooms, sliced

2 lbs. shrimp, peeled
4-5 garlic cloves, minced
1 cup green peas, frozen or canned
½ tsp. paprika
1 tbsp. fresh flat-leaf Italian parsley, chopped
Salt and pepper to taste

Fry potatoes in oil until browned or, if preferred, blanche in water and then brown in butter or olive oil.

Cut chicken into strips.

Melt ½ cup of butter in a large skillet. Add the chicken and brown lightly, then reserve.

Melt the remaining ¼ cup butter if needed in the same pan and sauté the mushrooms until they release their juices. Add the shrimp and sauté until pink, about 2 to 3 minutes. Lower the heat and add the garlic; cook for 2 to 3 minutes. Return the chicken to the pan and add the green peas and potatoes. Heat thoroughly. Sprinkle on paprika, parsley, salt, and pepper to taste.

Stuffed Shrimp

One of my favorite dishes on Dooky Chase's menu is Leah's stuffed shrimp. Using Chef Nathaniel Burton's recipe as inspiration, I cooked my first stuffed shrimp. The next day, I went to see Leah and told her, "Leah, I cooked Nathaniel Burton's stuffed shrimp last night, and it was absolutely delicious!" "What did you do?" Leah asked. I described the procedure and, in typical Leah fashion, she exclaimed, "That's not Nathaniel's recipe—that's mine!" Well, I've worked and reworked this one enough, so now I can say, "It's mine!"

Yields 6 servings

3 tbsp. butter
2 green onions, thinly sliced
2 tbsp. finely chopped celery
3 tbsp. finely chopped onion
1 tbsp. finely chopped flat-leaf parsley
1 lb. fresh crab claw meat
½ loaf French bread

3 eggs, divided
Salt and pepper to taste
4 cups plain, dry breadcrumbs, divided
3 lbs. fresh shrimp (about 36)
2 cups flour
1 cup milk
Oil for frying

Melt butter in a skillet, then add the green onions, celery, onion, and parsley. Sauté together for 10 minutes, or until soft. Add crabmeat and sauté for another 5 minutes.

Moisten French bread with water and chop finely. Add 2 eggs to bread and mix thoroughly. Add crabmeat mixture to egg and bread mixture and mix well; season with salt and pepper to taste. Add 2 to 3 tbsp. of the dry breadcrumbs so that stuffing is no longer sticky to the touch.

Peel and clean shrimp, leaving tails on. Butterfly each shrimp, then stuff with approximately 1 tbsp. of bread mixture.

Make an egg wash with 1 remaining egg and milk.

Roll each stuffed shrimp in flour, egg wash, and then remaining breadcrumbs.

Heat oil to 375 degrees and fry shrimp for about 5 minutes or until browned. Drain on paper towels and serve.

The Gorilla Man's Son

I am always surprised how the recording studio unexpectedly can feel like a confessional or a psychiatrist's office—how the earth suddenly begins to tilt for my guest as he or she considers a simple question with a complicated response.

The studio is a very private place, considering how public the conversations that take place there later become. Two microphones, two chairs facing each other, and my engineer, Thomas Walsh, seated just a few feet away at the soundboard. Thomas doesn't look at us. He listens through headsets, hearing the rough of what later will be edited for the radio audience.

When Randy Fertel served up to the world his 2011 memoir, *The Gorilla Man and the Empress of Steak,* it was as bloody and raw as any piece of rare meat his famous mother, Ruth Fertel of Ruth's Chris Steakhouse fame, ever placed on a sizzling platter. Randy had labored over the book for years, and the result was a ruthlessly brave,

personal examination of generations of wealthy, eccentric Fertels and the hardworking Plaquemines Parish folks who had formed him.

Kind, smiling, generous Randy is well known in philanthropic circles across the US. He has a natural, passionate interest in food projects, whether it involves the children of the Edible Schoolyard New Orleans, a seed he planted with Alice Waters post-Katrina, or the menhaden, a tiny fish that are an essential link in the Gulf's food chain endangered due to overfishing.

I couldn't wait to read Randy's book and was beyond thrilled when he agreed to grant me his first interview. I read his proof copy over a hot summer weekend at the fishing camp. Again and again, I found myself gasping out loud at some of his brutally honest revelations. No one was spared—not even Grandma Annie Fertel. Randy wrote that she had a great penchant for "five-fingered discount" shopping sprees, filling a giant shopping bag with trinkets from Canal Street department stores. Luckily, her great wealth and her attentive accountant paid the bills the stores would later submit to the accountant, claiming to have had the store detective follow her as she shopped—something that Randy believes managed to keep her out of jail, or at least the Southeast Louisiana State Mental Hospital. And this was just the tip of the Fertel-family iceberg.

Randy was late for our interview. As he is usually very punctual, I became concerned as time ticked by. Finally, he arrived and settled into the chair facing me. Once the microphones were adjusted and the sound check completed, he removed his glasses, rubbed his eyes, and gazed at the floor. It was in that moment that I clearly had the sensation that Randy felt as though he was either in a confessional or on a psychiatrist's couch.

His anxiety seemed palpable when I asked him why he felt this story needed to be told. "Well, I love New Orleans and I had this tiger by the tail—this amazing New Orleans story of my mother's founding of Ruth's Chris and my wacky father's run for mayor on the platform that the zoo needed a gorilla," he answered. "A lot of people knew their stories individually, but a lot of people did not know that they were once yoked together—and that I'm the fruit of that. So, it's that this icon of the business world—a woman—was once married to this man who was just as iconic, but not as quite as revered, was a story that I thought should be told. The funny thing about my mom was that she was incredibly reputable; she was a stickler for paying her bills on time, but she surrounded herself with rogues not unlike my dad, and that's the story that I wanted to tell."

Despite his illustrious college degrees and undeniable wealth, the grown man sitting across from me suddenly seemed to be the same self-described "Roly-Poly Randy,"

a fourth grader yanked out of the comfortable, private-school atmosphere of the Sam Barthe School for Boys and forced to attend the neighborhood public school when his parents separated. Included in the memoir was his school photo from that year, showing him complete with a little boy's cowlick, grinning bravely into the camera.

Listening to that interview now, I can hear the sadness of a little boy who didn't feel as if he fit in, unsure of the love of either parent. Looking across at him in the studio, I wanted to reach out and hug him just to let him know that, really, it was all going to be okay. At least, I hoped that it would be, knowing that the depth of the secrets he'd revealed were soon to become common knowledge to anyone who read his book.

As our conversation continued, Randy became more at ease, and we laughed about his travels with his dad when he was a teenager, about meeting Salvador Dalí and his ocelot, about eating caviar alone in the grand dining room of the Ritz-Carlton Hotel in Barcelona, and then about how at home, he worked for his mom at the original Ruth's Chris on North Broad Street as a busboy—one who didn't get to keep his own tips.

When I pointed out the societal dichotomy, he was momentarily speechless, then wisely quoted Faulkner: "The only story worth telling is the story of the heart's conflict with itself." He added, "You know, we're all complicated, and this is my complicated story."

As we continued, we discussed his Plaquemines Parish Grandmother Hingle's holiday dressing made with seventeen sacks of freshly shucked oysters, the dark roux of her gumbo, and Great Uncle Martin's creamed spinach, which lives on today as one of the most popular sides on the Ruth's Chris menu.

After about forty minutes, we concluded the interview,

and I got up to see Randy out. He turned to me and sheepishly acknowledged how late he'd arrived at the radio station. He explained that as this was his very first interview, on the drive out to the station, he'd suddenly gotten a little nervous about what I might ask and how the whole thing would unfold. He confided to me that he'd pulled over to the side of the road and called our mutual friend, Diana Pinckley.

Diana, PR maven, brilliant writer, and true friend always there to help, had been one of the essential midwives instrumental in helping Randy see this project to fruition. He'd called Diana for advice on how to handle the interview, concerned about how this would all turn out. Diana and I had long been friends as well, so according to Randy, when she heard his worried tone, she just laughed and said, "Randy! For goodness' sake, it's just Poppy!"

Randy left with a laugh saying "Now, if I can just get Terry Gross [of the popular NPR show *Fresh Air*] to interview me . . ."

Ruth's Garlicky White Remoulade

Randy was kind enough to share some recipes with me from his mother's Plaquemines Parish family, the Hingles. Standardized, commissary versions of the remoulade and creamed spinach (to follow) can still be found today on the tables of Ruth's Chris Steakhouse across the world.

A family recipe from Plaquemines Parish with roots in France, this remoulade sauce was changed a bit for Ruth's Chris. In New Orleans, there are two kinds of remoulade: red remoulade, which is full of paprika, cayenne, lemon, and olive oil, served at famous restaurants such as Galatoire's; and this more classically French one, a garlicky, mayonnaise-based, white remoulade. This is best made ahead of time so that the garlic marries with the other ingredients. Creole mustard is key here, but if you must, substitute with a grainy dark mustard.

Yields 2½ cups

1 15-oz. jar Hellmann's mayonnaise
4 oz. Zatarain's Creole mustard
3 cloves garlic or to taste
3 tbsp. lemon juice

½ tsp. Lea & Perrins Worcestershire sauce
¼ tsp. Tabasco sauce
3 tbsp. parsley, minced
2 green onions, minced

Place mayonnaise, mustard, garlic, lemon, Worcestershire sauce, and hot sauce in a blender or bowl. Combine well. Mix in minced parsley and green onions.

Refrigerate for at least a few hours before serving. Serve with boiled shrimp or any cold seafood.

Ruth's Chris Creole French Salad Dressing

The original Ruth's Chris Creole French Salad Dressing, created by Ruth Fertel in the early days of the famous steakhouse, has long been retired but is still remembered fondly by many early customers. The original "regular salad" was comprised of chopped iceberg lettuce, tomato wedges, and a canned white asparagus spear with a couple of anchovies draped on top. The following recipe is inspired by Randy's taste memories of the original.

Yields approximately 2 cups

½ cup red wine vinegar
½ tsp. salt
2 tsp. black pepper
1¼ tsp. sugar
1 tbsp. plus 1 tsp. paprika

1 tbsp. plus 1 tsp. yellow mustard
1 tbsp. Lea & Perrins Worcestershire sauce
1 tbsp. plus 2 tsp. Zatarain's Creole mustard
¼ cup finely grated Romano cheese
1 cup vegetable oil

Whisk all ingredients, except for the vegetable oil, together in a mixing bowl.

When well combined, slowly whisk in the vegetable oil until dressing is emulsified.

Store the dressing in a jar in the refrigerator.

Uncle Martin's Creamed Spinach

This is the recipe that inspired Ruth's Chris famous creamed spinach.

Yields 6 servings

3 lbs. frozen spinach, thawed, plus 1 1-lb. bag fresh baby spinach, divided
1 cup unsalted butter
½ cup flour

1 qt. half-and-half, divided
1½ tsp. salt
¼ tsp. white pepper
Dash nutmeg

Thaw frozen spinach thoroughly and cook in boiling water for 10 minutes. Remove from heat and drain, pressing water from spinach.

Melt butter in a large, heavy-bottomed pot or Dutch oven set over medium heat. Add flour and whisk constantly until mixture forms a light roux, about 3 minutes. Slowly whisk in 2 cups of the half-and-half, blending thoroughly. Season with salt and white pepper. Stir in fresh spinach, remaining half-and-half, and nutmeg. Heat thoroughly and serve.

Ruth Fertel's Plaquemines Parish Oyster Dressing

This delicious classic, oyster dressing is still a fixture on Fertel and Hingle Thanksgiving dinner tables. If your family isn't quite as large, this recipe is easily halved.

Yields 15-20 servings

1 gallon oysters with liquid
2½ cups butter, melted, divided
1 lb. smoked sausage, minced
1 lb. hot sausage, minced
3 cups diced onions
2 cups diced celery
1 cup diced green bell peppers

1 cup diced red bell peppers
¼ cup minced garlic
12 chicken bouillon cubes
3 stale poor boy bread or French bread loaves
1 dozen eggs, whipped
Salt, black pepper, and cayenne pepper to taste

Preheat oven to 350 degrees.

Pour oysters and the oyster liquid into a 5-quart pot. Check oysters to make sure that any shell pieces are removed. Gently poach oysters over a medium heat until edges begin to ruffle. Drain oysters, reserving all poaching liquid. When oysters are cool to the touch, coarsely chop them and set aside.

In a large Dutch oven, heat ½ cup of the butter over medium-high heat. Sauté sausages until browned and fat is rendered. Add onions, celery, bell peppers, and garlic. Sauté for 3 to 5 minutes or until vegetables are wilted.

Add chopped oysters, oyster liquid, and bouillon cubes. Bring to a rolling boil, reduce to a simmer, and cook together for 5 minutes.

Cut bread into 1" cubes and add bread into oyster mixture, 2 cups at a time, until enough bread has been added to absorb liquid but mixture is still moist. Remove from heat and add eggs, salt, black pepper, cayenne pepper, and the remaining 2 cups of butter, blending well. Pour into a large baking pan. Cover with aluminum foil and bake for 1 hour. Remove foil and brown for about 15 minutes.

The Ghost Whisperer and the Voodoo Priestess

Halloween has always been one of my favorite holidays. Especially in New Orleans, where we love to costume, Halloween has always been a sign that Mardi Gras is on its way!

From haunted plantations all along the Mississippi River to haunted restaurants, hotels, and bed and breakfasts, Louisiana must be one of the ghostliest states in the nation. With hundreds of years of fuel for the fodder, in the supernatural department, we are rife with material. The author Jessica Harris, who is a fully indoctrinated Candomblé voodoo priestess, makes New Orleans her sometimes home. With our ancient cemeteries and religious traditions, Jessica has described New Orleans as "a spiritual keyhole."

When my show was first on the air, I invited my longtime friend Priestess Miriam Chamani, who presides over North Rampart Street's Voodoo Spiritual Temple, to be a *Louisiana Eats!* guest. In eighteenth-century New Orleans, every Sunday the enslaved and free people of color from West Africa would gather to drum, dance, and trade native wares in a place that was called Congo Square. Today, Congo Square is known as Louis Armstrong Park, and Miriam's temple is just across the street from that traditional, sacred ground.

Miriam responded to my call by saying, "When you call me, then it's like magic!" We scheduled a studio interview to talk specifically about the use of herbs in voodoo practices. She swept into the studio, bracelets jangling, carrying a little bag of chicken bones I'd asked her to bring along. I'd had Miriam throw the bones for me before at the temple and thought it would make for entertaining radio if she did it there in the studio with me.

I began by asking her about the spiritual nature of herbs. She answered, "It's something natural that peoples have had to rely on when there was discomfort in their life—their health—and also for their environment—for fumigation, used for having some aroma to eradicate the unsettled energy that the peoples of the 1800s were going through. Today people need them for their emotional stresses. It's like an over-the-counter medicine today, but in those days it was the true natural pharmaceutical."

I asked what herbs she used, and she answered, "The herbs I use come in multiple sources. I use them according to the different order. The ideas that are taking place at the time—whether it's people's health or their love-life problems.

"Over the years, I've been looking at the magical expression of the African peoples who practice voodoo, managing their life and luck, finding something to improve their fortune. For the love life, which sometimes is tops over their health, it's amazing. You can use things right out of your kitchen. There is jasmine. You can have lavender or cinnamon. Ginger is a big herb that can be used to improve or empower your love. Heat it up, spice it up."

Her advice continued, "If there's sort of a low, lethargic energy and you feel like something has gone weak in the emotional structure of yourself and your partner, you just take a little cinnamon before your husband comes home and poof!" She gestured with her hands like the problem would be all solved.

When I asked about luck and money, Miriam said, "Many people walk around with the John the Conqueror root in their pocket along with many other herbs like lovash root. You'll find John the Conqueror root in pockets at the casino and the Devil's Shoestring! That's like a vine that you can use to make your powerful good luck hand and carry it with you for gambling or court situations. A four-leaf clover is said to keep your luck forever. It's good if you can put it in a dollar bill, fold it and hide it in your wallet.

"When you're traveling, you can put some comfrey in your luggage to keep it from getting lost. Put it in your luggage and take it wherever you're going and it's just like moving away a negative vibration."

Then I asked what a mojo bag was. I'd seen them for sale in the temple and had never inquired about them before. "A mojo bag is unique because it reminds you that you don't have to have fears or worries," Miriam said. "It's something to remind you that you got your luck. Many times, peoples are not able to just project themselves with their mind. They need a little tool to carry with them to help them, so when they arrive wherever they're going there's some trust and security in their mind—to be able to achieve the successes they want."

I asked Miriam if she'd throw the bones for us. She emptied the bag and, holding the chicken bones in her palms, she began to toss them slightly. The audio of those rattling bones made for some very special radio.

Miriam threw her hands apart and let the bones fall on the countertop in front of her. She said, "Many times, travelers will be going in and out of the villages and they want to get a sense of direction, wondering what's up and what's ahead of us now, my brother.

"The old African priest will be sitting there and he'll be rattling his bones. He'll say 'Well, why don't you just sit down with me here for a moment, so that you can see your wits before you get farther on up the road.' And then, the African priest throws the bones. 'Ah my brother, I think you should delay for a moment and maybe just sleep over here with me through the night and then when you rise in the morning, then your future looks bright and you can go forward on your way.'"

I asked Miriam what she saw in the future for me and for *Louisiana Eats!,* and she answered, "I believe that you are on a very good wave of energy and it's the time."

When I read about Mary Ann Winkowski's *The Ghost Whisperer's Cookbook* in the *New Orleans Times-Picayune* in October 2011, it was too late to book her for our *Louisiana Eats!* Halloween show that year, so I had to wait a year before I finally got to speak with her in 2012. In the meantime, I read her first book, *When Ghosts Speak.* I thought maybe Mary Ann could even help me understand the ghostly woes of another *Louisiana Eats!* guest, Chef Greg Picolo.

Loving the supernatural as I do, the previous year I had interviewed Greg at his restaurant in the French Quarter, the Bistro at Maison de Ville. He had been putting up with a variety of ghosts from several different time periods who hung around there and had even caused staffing problems by scaring some of his kitchen employees right off the line during dinner service. Unfortunately, the Bistro at the Maison de Ville is no more, but we suspect that the ghostly residents of the establishment are still present.

For some reason, there was a lot of chaos at the station when I arrived the day I had scheduled the interview with Mary Ann. Not only had Thomas been pulled onto a different project, but also the usual studio space was not available either. I had to apologize once I finally got her on the line with the station's *All Things Considered* host, Jack Hopke, sitting in for Thomas as emergency engineer.

I began by asking Mary Ann when she first remembered being able to communicate with spirits. She told me about seeing a ghost in the school hallways when she was seven. Like a good Catholic girl, she had asked the nun who that "creepy, hobo-looking guy standing behind my classmate in the hall was." The nun had chastised her and told her that it must be a guardian angel.

But Mary Ann had seen enough guardian angel photos to know that the dirty guy with the missing teeth was not likely to be one. Complaining a second time just got her in trouble. The nun, who she now refers to as Sister Mary Altar Cloth, bypassed the principal and sent Mary Ann straight to the priest, who threatened that if she didn't stop telling these stories, she wouldn't be able to receive her first communion later that year.

Mary Ann's grandparents were Italians who barely spoke English. They lived in an immigrant Ohio neighborhood full of Polish, Irish, and Hungarian transplants. Her grandmother would often receive visits from the old country in the form of dreams—friends and relatives of friends of all nationalities who had died and wanted to let her neighbors know. "Grandma would wake up, go across the street and say, 'Rose, your brother Luigi died last night.' Sure enough, in a week or so, the letter would come confirming the death," Mary Ann remembered.

When she was four, Mary Ann stayed with her grandparents while her mother gave birth to a sibling. When her grandma found little Mary Ann standing alone in the sunroom animatedly speaking Italian into thin air, she asked, "Who are you talking to?" When Mary Ann explained she was talking to "the nice man," her grandmother realized that, different from her own psychic abilities, little Mary Ann could see and talk with spirits when she was awake.

That's why, at the age of four, she began accompanying her grandmother to funerals. Mary Ann advised me that people should be very careful at funerals. According to her, the dead have between seventy-two and eighty hours after their service to "go into the light," and if they miss that opportunity, "they remain stuck here on earth." She reports that you should be very careful what you say and do at funerals, because the deceased is often there in attendance, standing at the foot of the coffin, watching and hearing every word.

During our interview, Mary Ann explained that it's

those earthbound spirits "who cause problems in people's houses. They don't eat or sleep but they need human energy to keep them going. So they make problems in order to get their energy from stressed out, upset people."

She continued to describe these spirits as a "total energy drain. They're energy vampires. They suck the energy out of you. They get you to fight with your spouse and kids. If there are children in the house under the age of ten or twelve, these kids are going to constantly have ear, nose, and throat issues—upper respiratory problems. These are the kids who don't like their bedrooms in the middle of the night. At two in the morning, they're going to be in bed with you. With adults, it can be totally unexplained headaches when they're home, maybe lower intestinal disturbances.

"I do more houses with divorce because of earthbound spirits than anything else," she revealed, but then assured me that "most people don't know the ghost in their house, because your own relatives wouldn't do that to you!

"They are anywhere. They like to be where there is a crowd of people, like malls, theaters, stadiums, restaurants, and grocery stores. Think how stressed out we are when we run into a grocery for just one thing. Believe it, they are there. They're not in cemeteries—everybody there is dead."

I asked if these spirits were actually capable of moving objects as I'd heard they do. She said, "They have more energy during the week leading up to a full moon, causing all hell to break loose in restaurants and bars," something she described as similar to feeding time at the zoo.

"I don't know why, but as the moon phase increases, they begin to be able to move jewelry, a remote control, a garage door opener, coffee cups, keys, bills . . ."

I'd read in her book that she could detect ghosts over the phone, so I asked if there was a spirit hanging around the radio station. "There is a woman in," she paused, "like a kitchen area. Actually, why do you have two coffee pots in there? She's not very old, maybe forty-five, and is dressed like maybe she died in the early 1990s. Of course, maybe she never worked there herself, but belongs to someone there who does and she just comes to work with them every day."

Weirdly enough, after we finished the interview, I investigated the station's little efficiency kitchen and there was one coffee pot in use sitting out on the counter and a second one on a lower shelf.

Despite how much I was enjoying the spirit talk, I reminded Mary Ann that we had to get to the topic of food, because the name of the show is *Louisiana Eats!,* after all. I asked how she began getting recipes from ghosts.

She recalled the first recipe she'd gotten. She went to see an older lady who was having problems in her house. "When I got there, it smelled so good!" Mary Ann recalled. "She had freshly baked nut rolls cooling on the counter." When Mary Ann remarked on the delicious smell, the ghost, whom she already had spotted standing there, said, "Oh yeah, they smell good, but they taste terrible! She has no idea how to make a nut roll."

Mary Ann claims that, in her work, she has the ability to "make people go into the light," so that's what she was there for. She asked the ghost, "Are you ready to go into the light?" The ghost agreed to go if Mary Ann would write down the ghost's special nut roll recipe, complete with a hint on how to roll it out in a special way on a pastry cloth.

Observing Mary Ann's scribbling, the lady who owned the house asked her, "What did you write down?" Mary Ann said, "I told her the ghost was so happy you brought me here to release her that she wanted me to give you her secret nut roll recipe. Would you like it?"

The homeowner said yes and thanked her for it. A few weeks later, she called Mary Ann to say, "Everybody is asking me for that recipe the ghost gave you! No one had ever asked for my recipe before."

Sometimes, I will do a recipe segment on *Louisiana Eats!,* and for one of the Halloween shows I did a piece about New Orleans most famous voodoo priestess, Marie Laveau. It shouldn't come as a surprise that it all had to do with gumbo!

Marie was a devout Catholic, and through her friendship with St. Louis Cathedral's Père Antoine, she was allowed to minister to condemned men imprisoned in the state prison on Pirate's Alley. She frequently spent the night before an execution with them. Marie would erect an altar and provide them with a last supper of gumbo, which she promised would be "a gumbo such as you have never eaten in your life."

On July 17, 1850, Jean Adam and Anthony Delisle were condemned to hang for the murder of a young mulatto servant girl. They both experienced Marie Laveau's gumbo for their last supper. On that bright, cloudless day, hundreds gathered to witness their execution.

Just before the men were to hang, a deluge of rain suddenly drenched the assembled, including Marie Laveau, who stood at the foot of the gallows. As the trapdoor opened for the men to drop to their deaths, they slipped through the nooses, falling to the ground and thwarting the hangman's efforts. All who witnessed the spectacle were certain that it was the work of the voodoo queen.

The hanging was attempted a second time later and was successful, but because of the particularly gruesome nature of what took place that day, Louisiana became the first state in the nation to ban public executions.

As you walk the streets of the Vieux Carré or perhaps visit Marie's grave in St. Louis Cemetery No. 2, you may come across a bowl of gumbo ringed by shiny silver coins. For more than 150 years, the faithful have believed this to be an appropriate offering to Marie Laveau, New Orleans' iconic voodoo queen.

Poppy's Seafood Gumbo

Now, I don't claim to know Marie Laveau's gumbo recipe. But when you're ready to make an offering to her, you can just use mine. I did beat Bobby Flay in a "throwdown" with this gumbo, and on *CBS Sunday Morning*, it made jazz trumpeter Wynton Marsalis implore, "Have mercy, Poppy!" Whether or not this is the original, Marie Laveau just might be satisfied with a big bowl of this.

Yields 10-12 servings

2 lbs. shrimp, shells and heads on
1 onion, chopped, peel reserved
3 stalks celery, chopped, tops and bottoms reserved
6-8 green onions, thinly sliced, parings reserved
1 pt. oysters
2 lbs. okra, sliced into ¼" rounds
½ cup oil, plus additional for frying
1 cup flour

1 bell pepper, chopped
1 lb. gumbo crabs
1 1-lb. can crushed tomatoes
2 tbsp. thyme
1 bay leaf
1 clove garlic, minced
Salt and pepper to taste
Hot sauce to taste

Peel shrimp, reserving heads and shells. Make a stock by combining shrimp heads and peels, onion skins, celery bottoms and tops, and green onion parings in a stock pot. Cover with water in excess of 2" over discards and boil for 15 minutes. Strain and reserve liquid.

Drain oysters and reserve oyster liquor; set aside.

Fry okra in very hot oil until lightly browned.

Make a dark roux with the flour and ½ cup oil, cooking to the color of milk chocolate. Add chopped onions, stirring until the roux darkens to a bittersweet chocolate brown. Add celery and bell pepper. Sauté for 5 minutes, then add the gumbo crabs, tomatoes, okra, thyme, bay leaf, shrimp stock, and oyster liquor. Add garlic and salt and pepper to taste. Simmer for 45 minutes or longer.

Ten minutes before serving, add shrimp and green onions. Add hot sauce and salt as needed. Serve on top of cooked rice.

Calas

The calas recipe has an important tie in to the Congo Square part of our story. In the days before the Louisiana Purchase, New Orleanians were ruled by the Code Noir, the regulations that governed how white people, free people of color, and slaves were to live together in the city. The Code Noir stated that all slaves were required a day off. So, on their day off, which was often Sunday, many slaves spent the day at Congo Square, often selling food to the other Africans who gathered there. The proceeds earned helped some buy freedom for themselves and their families.

Calas came from Africa. In fact, today, if you visit the open-air markets of Ghana and Liberia, you can find the women there making calas. If you ask them, "What is that?" in their native Bantu tongue, they will answer, "Calas." This ancient dish made the trip across the Atlantic Ocean and kept its own name once it arrived in New Orleans, where it is still called calas today.

Yields 1 dozen

2 cups rice, cooked and cooled
6 tbsp. flour
3 heaping tbsp. sugar
2 tsp. baking powder
¼ tsp. salt

2 eggs, beaten
¼ tsp. vanilla
Vegetable oil, for deep-frying
Confectioners' sugar, for serving

In a bowl, combine rice, flour, sugar, baking powder, and salt. Mix well to coat rice with the dry ingredients. Add eggs and vanilla and mix to form a tight batter.

Heat vegetable oil for deep-frying to 360 degrees. Carefully drop rice mixture by spoonfuls into hot oil and fry until brown. Remove from oil with a slotted spoon and drain on paper towels. Sprinkle with confectioners' sugar. Serve hot.

The Candy Man Cometh

I remember hearing the ship's bell ringing as I sat on my grandparent's front porch in Broadmoor, a certain harbinger of the Roman Candy Man on his way down Fontainebleau Drive.

The cart's window seemed so high from where I stood in the street with my grandfather, the mule so tall. I dimly recall seeing the face of a pleasant old gentleman who appeared relatively low in the cart's window, as if perhaps he were seated. but my focus was always on the long, waxed-paper-wrapped sticks in shiny shades of pink, white, and brown—Roman taffy candy.

Virtually every New Orleans resident of the twentieth century shares some form of that sweet memory with me—but what very few knew was that the candy man in the window had no legs. The star of that memory was Sam Cortese, the original Roman Candy Man. I remember buying candy from a different, handsome, young Roman Candy Man on the Fairgrounds at the Jazz Fest years later, when I was in my late teens, and

even taking a photo with him that now has been lost with time.

Ronnie Kottemann's parents intended for him to go to college and pursue a traditional profession. Instead, Ronnie dropped out of college after a year and was drafted into service during the Vietnam War. While Ronnie was away in the military, his grandfather died. Until Ronnie was discharged two years later, New Orleans was without Roman candy. Ronnie came home and bought his grandparent's house, including the stable, the cart, and the mule. Eventually, he raised his own family there. Ronnie's Uptown house is the last one in the area with a stable, and he chuckles that it was "grandfathered" in city regulations—rather ironic, considering its origins.

When *Louisiana Eats!* first went into production, the interview I was dying to do from day one was with Ronnie Kottemann, the Roman Candy Man. I especially hoped that I would actually get to ride along in the wagon.

Ronnie agreed, and Thomas Walsh, my sound engineer,

met me on St. Charles Avenue lugging the station's recording equipment. We climbed up into the cart and the mule pulled out into the afternoon traffic. Ronnie pulled taffy, cutting the shiny strands into uniform lengths and wrapping them into precut rectangles of waxed paper on the same white marble slab his grandfather had used.

Amazingly, the mule knew her own way up Octavia Street towards Isidore Newman School, a regular afternoon route for her and the candy man. As we meandered along, accompanied by the sound of the mule's hooves on the street, the cart slightly swaying, I asked Ronnie to tell the story of his grandfather, Sam Cortese.

He began: "In the early 1900s, when Grandpa was a boy of just ten years old, he was run over by a streetcar, losing both of his legs. When his legs healed and he went back to school, they considered him to be a problem because he had to be carried around. He drove a little goat cart back and forth to school and sometimes the kids would let the goats loose in the school." Ronnie chuckled at the thought. "Goats running through the classrooms weren't appreciated by the administration, so they kicked him out."

Booted out of school in the third grade, little Sam had to do something, so he took the goat cart, put some fruit and vegetables on it, and went out peddling. "From the time he was twelve years old, he was a peddler," Sam's grandson said proudly.

"After a while, he got into the stone coal business. Houses had no electricity or gas back then. Everything was done by fireplace, so Grandpa sold stone coal in the winter and fruit and vegetables in the summer, eventually moving into a full-sized wagon instead of the goat cart."

Sam's mother, Angelina Napoli, was a Sicilian immigrant. She had a family recipe for taffy that she'd brought with her from Italy, one she had learned from her own mother and grandmother. This style of candy traveled to the island of Sicily with the Phoenicians, who established a trading post there in 800 BC. The Phoenicians took it along on long sea voyages and chewed it between meals to clean their teeth. Angelina made it for special celebrations such as Christmas, New Year's, and St. Joseph's Day, and when there was any left over, Sam would take it out on the route.

"When people started asking for it, in 1915, Grandpa decided to give selling candy a shot instead of fruit and vegetables," Ronnie continued. "So he went around to several wheelwrights showing them the design for the new candy cart he had in mind. They all told him it couldn't be done, except for one guy named Tom Brinker."

Brinker had a shop on Washington and Claiborne Avenues where, together, Sam and the wheelwright planned and built the original cart that Ronnie still uses today—New Orleans' original food truck! There are no wheelwrights left in New Orleans now, so Ronnie has taught himself that craft as well in order to keep the original cart rolling on wooden wheels.

"What made the cart so unusual back then was that Grandpa wanted glass all around, and windows were very seldom seen. Usually, carts used canvas that was rolled up or down depending on the weather—but he wanted the people to see him making the candy inside of the wagon," Ronnie explained.

"Also, he needed a way to drive from the inside of the wagon, so he could drive and make candy at the same time. The vast majority of wagons and carts and carriages had a perch where the driver would sit outside with passengers or cargo riding inside." Sam arranged to hold the reins inside the windowed cart, allowing him to control the mule and make candy at the same time.

Initially, Sam made the candy using a coal-fired stove. Ronnie laughed, "I can only imagine how that worked!" When Sam started the business, each stick of candy cost just a nickel.

The Roman Candy business has been run out of 5510 Constance Street since its earliest days. When Sam became engaged to Ronnie's grandmother, he purchased the Constance Street property for them to live in and to house the business.

Alongside the narrow shotgun house, originally built in the 1880s, is a stable built at the same time. "The business is run today exactly as it was back then. It's unusual nowadays, but if you look at old New Orleans houses with a long driveway and a shed in the back that has three cars in it now, that was a stable at one time. That's not a garage, that's a converted stable," Ronnie said.

Sam worked certain routes, covering much more of the city than Ronnie does today. Ronnie recalls that his grandfather would go "from the western boundary—the Causeway—and east across the Industrial Canal and into the Ninth Ward and Chalmette. He'd go from the lake all the way across the river to Algiers and Gretna. They had ramps then that were built for horse and wagon with slats on them, so the horses could catch the slats with their feet and they wouldn't slip."

Ronnie's mother, Angelina Cortese, was the only daughter of a brood of eleven. She married Ronnie's father, Robert Kottemann Sr., and had eleven children herself. Ronnie reminisced: "When the first four of us got to be teenagers, my brothers and I got a little truck and went around selling Roman candy, popcorn, peanuts, and cotton candy. We knew where Grandpa was going so we just stayed out of that area because it was no use trying to compete with him anyway. All the ice cream people in the business knew—if they saw Grandpa, they just

headed for a different part of town because it was just no use." Within four or five years, the truck business earned enough to pay for the Kottemann brothers' education.

"Then, about the time I was getting ready to go to college, we got rid of the truck and I just started working with Grandpa exclusively, especially during the summer," Ronnie continued. "And I liked it—it's a good business. It's physically demanding, but it's something different every day. You meet new people all the time. It's interesting—not like sitting behind a desk."

The day Ronnie took us for a ride on the wagon, the mule was named Ada. He'd had Ada for only a few months, and said, "She's a smart mule and she looks like she's going to work out just fine."

Rose was Ronnie's favorite mule ever. His eyes still light up when he talks about her. "She was the most intelligent animal of any kind I ever encountered. If you showed her how to do something twice, that was it. She had it down pat, that was the end of it," he said.

"She was really something special. She knew all the routes in the city. You never really had to touch the reins. It was all voice command. She knew which houses had regular customers and she would stop and wait for them to come out.

"Rose could parallel park," Ronnie claimed. He remembered the first time he took her downtown. He maneuvered her into a spot as the cars moved around them in the busy street. But once they got in the spot, he said, "She looked all around and was like, 'Man, that was cool.' After that, if Rose knew there was a spot there, you could pull up, point her towards the car and just pull the reins back to let her back up; and then, let her go and she would just parallel park right in that spot." With a wicked look, he finished by saying, "One of the few females in this city who knows how to parallel park!"

As we maneuvered the narrow, one-lane Uptown street, a kid yelled out, "I want some candy!" Ronnie stopped the wagon and asked, "Chocolate, vanilla, or strawberry?" The little boy made his choice, and Ronnie handed down a stick of Roman taffy candy, saying with a smile and a wave, "Thanks! Have a nice day!"

This was my first ride on the wagon with Ronnie, but Ronnie and I were old friends by then. Back at the start of our friendship, I sometimes worried that he would think I was a crazy stalker. When the Slow Food Ark of Taste talk revved up in New Orleans in 1999, the local chapter joined my enthusiasm for bestowing the Ark designation on our treasured Roman candy. That was when I first approached Ronnie, explaining the special distinction the international organization was willing to bestow upon him and his historic candy.

The mule delivered Ronnie and the wooden cart to the door of Susan Spicer's business, Spice, Inc., a cooking school that she operated for a time in the then-newly gentrified Warehouse District. The just-formed Slow Food New Orleans chapter had unanimously nominated and voted our taffy candy onto the Slow Food USA's Ark of Taste, and Ronnie was there to be honored.

In order to qualify for boarding onto the virtual Noah's Ark that is Slow Food's Ark of Taste, a food must have important cultural and historical ties to a particular area, be produced in an authentic, traditional way, and be endangered. The fact that Ronnie is the sole maker and purveyor of this traditional New Orleans treat dating back more than a century made the qualification process easy. That is how Roman taffy candy became one of the very first products to officially board the Slow Food USA Ark of Taste.

When Hurricane Katrina struck, Slow Food friends across the country raised funds to help restore New Orleans' essential historic food producers. The relief effort was sort of an organic movement that began in California with the Sonoma chapter and spread like wildfire across the country.

The Slow Food USA executive director at the time, Erika Lesser, asked if I would administer the distribution of funds. I agreed, on the condition that the fund would not have the name "Katrina" tied to it. At my request, Slow Food USA called the fund the "Terra Madre Relief Fund" in a nod to Slow Food founder Carlo Petrini's vision of Mother Earth as ultimately being humanity's most vital link. Without caring for Mother Earth (*terra madre*), who provides us with the nourishment needed to live, mankind is surely doomed.

Most of the funds went to farmers and fishermen, as Richard McCarthy, the founder and executive director of the Crescent City Farmers Market, and I did our best to determine both the level of need and ability to rebuild the individual businesses, but some of those monies were used to help raise a new roof on the stable of the Roman Candy Man's mule. The original roof had been blown off in the hurricane and Patsy, the mule, had been exiled to a Northshore farm until repairs could be made.

In 2006, when Patsy, Ronnie's mule, finally pulled the wagon out onto the city's streets, the traditional ringing of the ship's bell announced the return of Roman taffy candy. Cell phones across the city lit up as New Orleans natives reported on the special bite of life that had returned to the city's streets.

Vanilla Pull Taffy

No one knows the exact candy recipe except for Ronnie. As a teenager, I learned to make a simple formula from one of my mother's cookbooks. Here's my adaptation of a classic taffy recipe.

Yields ½ lb.

1¼ cups sugar
¼ cup water
2 tbsp. white vinegar

1½ tsp. butter
½ tsp. vanilla

Combine sugar, water, vinegar, and butter in a saucepan and stir over low heat until the sugar is dissolved. Then, without stirring, increase the heat to medium-high to cook quickly to the very hard-ball stage (between 268 and 270 degrees Fahrenheit). Add vanilla and pour out onto a cold, buttered surface.

When the mixture is soft enough that you can press a dent on the surface with your finger, gather mixture into a ball and pull in foot-long lengths until taffy is light and shiny. Roll into long, thin strips and cut into 1" pieces. Store in a tightly covered container.

One of These Days, I'm Going to Go in That Restaurant

Racial segregation in New Orleans restaurants and other public places finally came to an end in 1963 with a Supreme Court ruling in the *Lombard vs. Louisiana* case. The long march to the highest court in the nation had begun when Rudy Lombard and two friends took a seat at McCrory's five-and-dime lunch counter on Canal Street.

Segregation was a well-respected "tradition," dating back to the 1876 Jim Crow laws of Recontructionist America, later overruled by the Civil Rights Act of 1964. But in New Orleans of 1963, Mayor deLesseps Story "Chep" Morrison did his best to uphold the "tradition," ordering that "no additional sit-in demonstrations or so-called peaceful picketing . . . will be permitted," and commanding police to enforce this by repeatedly arresting and jailing any demonstrators.

Rudy Lombard lives in Chicago now, but after meeting him through our mutual friend Leah Chase, I finally got him into the WWNO recording studio to talk about issues of food and race.

I asked Rudy what propelled him into action. "I think for me it began with my mother, Delores Lombard. She cooked for one of the wealthy families in New Orleans, the John Stewart family. They lived on the corner of Dryades and Napoleon across the street from one of the better-known restaurants, Manale's," he said.

In 1944, when Rudy was five years old and his mother, Delores, began working for the Stewarts in their plantation-style Uptown home, the journey to Delores' job required a ride across the Mississippi River on the segregated Algiers Ferry to Canal Street. From there, they took a segregated St. Charles Avenue streetcar the rest of the way.

From that young age, Rudy's palate was informed by "what all the rich, white people ate." Dolores was an ingenious, intuitive cook who could reproduce almost any dish described to her. Even elaborate restaurant specialties such as flaming Crêpes Suzette were part of her repertoire, making Delores an invaluable asset to her employers.

Today, Rudy realizes that even some of the specialties his mom cooked at home originated in those white Uptown kitchens. He believes that's where her penchant for canned white asparagus salad dressed with a simple vinaigrette materialized.

While his mother worked, Rudy was free to roam the Stewarts' backyard and the servant quarters above the garage where, because of the demands of her schedule, Dolores and Rudy would sometimes spend the night. But more often than not, in the early evening twilight, Rudy and his mother would head home, passing Pascal's Manale Restaurant. The brilliant neon light of the popular eatery called attention to a place renowned for the cold, raw oysters and spicy barbeque shrimp for which the restaurant is still famous today.

"I was curious as hell about what went on at Manale's, and I knew as a kid that blacks were not allowed to go in there. I resolved that one of those days I was going to go in that restaurant," Rudy told me.

"I accompanied my mother all through the Garden District because in that very wealthy neighborhood, most of the people who did the cooking were blacks. The men were waiters and chauffeurs and so forth. Most of the cooks at that time were women. So I got to see these extraordinary people who were cooking in the back of the house, so to speak, and it stayed with me.

"Of course, everybody in my family, including my father, who had gone to cooking school on the GI bill, knew how to cook, but my mother was so terrific that he wouldn't dare go near the kitchen when she was alive. He worked the graveyard shift at the Marine Hospital up on Nashville. He came home at seven o'clock in the morning and all his friends gathered in the kitchen. Of course, my mother had food for them.

"Before my mother started working fulltime for various white families as a domestic, we were used to eating three different meals a day. She was a gourmet cook because of the time she spent cooking in the Garden District. And in the summer, we would go with that white family to Mississippi, to the beachfront communities, places like Waveland. Those were the only conditions which would allow the blacks to be on those beaches, because the black servants could take their families with them if they were going on that beach with the white families," he remembered.

Despite Delores' demanding schedule, the Lombard family never missed a meal at their Newton Street home in Algiers. Somehow, she managed to see that three full meals were served at home every day, always accompanied by fresh French bread, hot from one of three nearby neighborhood bakeries. The seasons dictated her gumbos. She cooked okra gumbo from late spring through early fall, redolent with tomato, fresh and smoked sausage, shrimp, crabs, oysters, and occasionally the chicken feet that Dolores loved. In winter, filé powder replaced the okra with much the same list of ingredients, except she never put tomatoes in her filé gumbo.

Of course, red beans and rice were always served on Mondays, flavored with pickle meat (pickled pork) from the neighborhood butcher. Dolores' spaghetti was a family favorite, and although the red gravy always began with fried pork chops, it could include meatballs or wieners and usually a few hard-boiled eggs. Her fried chicken was legendary, made by flouring the chicken pieces in a paper bag before frying it in her big, deep cast-iron pot until it was crispy and golden brown. Fried chicken was usually accompanied by potato salad, but sometimes her steakhouse-sized French fries made it extra special.

When Rudy graduated from high school in 1957, he

headed north to the University of Michigan. Despite his parents' protests, he left college after just one year and returned home to become a longshoreman. His college costs were too high for his parents to afford. While in the longshoremen's union, Rudy first began to take an interest in political action.

In 1960, when four students from North Carolina Agricultural and Technical State University held a sit-in at the Woolworth's lunch counter in Greensboro, North Carolina, Rudy doubted that such an event could take place in New Orleans. "Frankly, I thought the New Orleans police were too mean to allow that here," he said.

But the Congress of Racial Equality (CORE) helped Rudy and some Southern University students organize a local New Orleans CORE group. After completing some nonviolence training, they decided that in September 1960, they would stage a sit-in in downtown New Orleans.

"The first one we did was at Woolworth's, at the corner of Canal and Rampart, and the second one, we sat-in at the lunch counter at McCrory's. It was myself, Oretha Castle Haley, Cecil Carter, and a white student from Tulane by the name of Lanny Goldfinch. We were arrested and we had this policy—Jail No Bail—to help bring attention to the issues here," Rudy recalled.

Oretha Haley, like Rudy, wouldn't leave the jail—even after her aunt died. Rudy was allowed to talk with her and told her, "I'm cool, everything will be fine—everything is okay. You can go to your aunt's funeral. I'll see you on the outside." Only then did Oretha agree to leave.

Rudy's deep, personal interest in food and the people who cooked it later led the civil rights activist to write a 1978 cookbook chronicling the life stories and recipes of fifteen black master chefs who created the classic dishes that are the bedrock of New Orleans' cuisine. Co-authored by Chef Nathanial Burton, *Creole Feast* was dedicated to Dolores and Warren Lombard, Rudy's parents, whose influence can be traced from his birth to the lunch counter sit-ins and, ultimately, to the publication of this seminal work.

The story of how Rudy found Nathaniel Burton is a fascinating one. "A couple of years before I wrote the book, I was involved in an urban planning study," Rudy told me. "The Claiborne Avenue Design Team was meant to revitalize the culture of downtown New Orleans along Claiborne Avenue, because the I-10 expressway had destroyed the cultural function of Claiborne Avenue. It was the place where there had been the largest cluster of live oak trees in America. I-10 had destroyed black businesses, introduced blight to the area, and destroyed many of the traditional rituals that took place there at times like Carnival."

As Rudy reflected on New Orleans' cultural history with regard to the Claiborne Avenue study, he began to examine how "everything that was unique about New Orleans could be traced to the black presence in this city, whether it was music, whether it was Carnival, whether it was architecture and food."

Rudy could name specific people who had been influential in each of these areas, but when it came to food, he realized that he could not name names. He only knew that there were blacks cooking in all of the great restaurants in New Orleans. He figured that if he didn't know, very few people did.

Rudy mentioned this to his friend, Freddie Kohlman, a jazz drummer who knew Warren Leruth, the white chef of the great Leruth's Restaurant. Freddie introduced Rudy to Warren, and when Rudy asked him who was the greatest chef in New Orleans, without hesitation Warren said, "Hands down, Nathaniel Burton. If you can get to Nat Burton—he's trained at least fifty-six other chefs—he's the godfather of all the New Orleans chefs, black or white. If you can get to him—that's the key and that unlocks the treasure."

Burton was a black man from Mississippi who started working in New Orleans restaurants as a dishwasher and taught himself to cook by stepping in when other cooks would call in sick. By the time Rudy met Burton, he had been the executive chef at Commander's Palace and was then the executive chef at Broussard's.

Rudy called Burton and told him what he wanted to do. The great chef immediately agreed. "Let's do it!" he said. And that was how *Creole Feast* became the first book about America's professional chefs, before the concept of celebrity became so intertwined with a chef's success.

Together, Burton and Rudy settled on which chefs to profile. Rudy interviewed each of them and, in so doing, preserved forever the stories of the black men and women who had forged the roots of Creole restaurant cuisine.

"What I am thankful for to the great almighty God was that we did this at a time when we captured the aesthetics of culinary arts in New Orleans, many of which have now disappeared, like Corrine Dunbar's. We got to talk about people like Miss Leone Victor who created all of those recipes, who had died right before we got to Corrine Dunbar's to do this book. But, I met Thelma Elsey and people like that who Miss Victor had trained.

"The owner at the time was the nephew of the woman who started it, Mrs. Corrine Dunbar, and he told me, 'I come to New Orleans once a year. I travel all over the world and do damn near whatever I want to do. Those black people operate that restaurant, order the food, plan the menu, cook the food, entertain the guests and put the money in my bank account. I trust them implicitly—I don't think they've ever stolen a penny from me. I wouldn't know diddiley about how to run that restaurant!'"

In reflecting now on the chefs he met when writing *Creole Feast,* Rudy said, "You will never meet more kind, generous, and loving people than the men and women in that book. Austin Leslie, Leah Chase, they're the epitome of that."

As for me, I've never met a more kind, generous, and loving man than my friend Rudy Lombard.

Delores Lombard's Cream of Oyster Soup

Rudy suspects that the origins of a very rich and elegant cream of oyster soup, a particular favorite of his father, may have been the Uptown Stewart family's dining room table. Somehow, that soup inspired Rudy's dad, Warren Lombard, to host a annual "Hobo Dinner" for the neighborhood homeless. Warren would round them up and have them bathe and dress in fresh clothes that he provided before ceremoniously sitting them down at the Lombard kitchen table. Rudy made a special note that his mother, Delores, would set the table for the "hobos" with the formality expected uptown, complete with two lit candles.

Yields 4 servings

1 pt. oysters	2 stalks celery, finely chopped
½ cup butter	1 tsp. finely chopped fresh parsley
4 tbsp. flour	2 cups half-and-half
1 onion, minced	Salt and pepper to taste

Drain all oyster liquor from oysters and reserve.

In a 4-quart saucepan, melt the butter and whisk in the flour, cooking together over medium heat for 5 minutes until the flour is fully cooked. Add the onion, celery, and parsley, continuing to stir constantly for another 5 minutes until the onions are translucent. Whisk in oyster liquor and cream. Do not allow soup to boil or the cream will curdle. Cook over medium-low heat for 20 minutes.

Just before serving, add the raw oysters and cook until the edges begin to curl. Season with salt and pepper to taste. Serve immediately with hot, buttered French bread.

Spaghetti à la Lombard

Delores would only use No. 4 spaghetti for this Lombard family favorite. This is an "anything goes" type of recipe, where you may add wieners or meatballs to the sauce if desired.

Yields 4 servings

4 thin, bone-in pork chops
4 tbsp. vegetable oil
1 onion, chopped
2 stalks celery, chopped
1 4-oz. can tomato paste
1 tsp. dried thyme
1 tsp. dried basil
2 bay leaves
1 tbsp. chopped, fresh parsley
1 12-oz. can tomato sauce
4 cloves garlic, coarsely chopped
¼ tsp. sugar
Salt and pepper to taste
4 hard-boiled eggs, peeled
1 lb. No. 4 spaghetti, cooked according to package directions

In a 4-quart deep skillet, fry pork chops in oil until browned on both sides. Remove the pork chops and set aside.

Add the onion and celery to the remaining oil and rendered pork fat and sauté until translucent. Add the tomato paste, thyme, basil, bay leaves, and parsley to the vegetables in the pan and sauté together over medium heat for 5 minutes to deepen the flavor. Add the tomato sauce and garlic and simmer for 20 minutes.

Cut the pork chops into bite-sized pieces. Add to the sauce and simmer for another 20 minutes. Add sugar, salt, and pepper. Add hard-boiled eggs and cook until heated through. Serve sauce over spaghetti.

Stewed Chicken

Another classic from the Lombard family dinner table.

Yields 4 servings

1 5-lb. stewing hen, cut into pieces
Salt and pepper to taste
¼ cup vegetable oil
½ cup flour
2 onions, chopped
4 cups water

3 cloves garlic, coarsely chopped
1 tbsp. chopped fresh parsley
1 tsp. thyme
1 cup rice, cooked according to package directions

Season the chicken pieces with salt and pepper.

Add the oil to a large, deep skillet and heat until smoking. Add the chicken pieces and brown on both sides. Reduce heat and cover for 25 minutes, checking periodically to ensure that nothing sticks or burns. Remove the chicken pieces and set aside.

Add the flour to the remaining oil and stir together over low heat until golden brown. Add the onions and continue cook until translucent. Add the water and bring to a boil, stirring to remove any bits that may be sticking to the pan. Add the garlic, parsley, and thyme to the gravy. Add the chicken back into the pan and cover. Cook over low heat for about 45 minutes, or until chicken is tender. Serve over rice.

Potato Salad

One of the tricks of preparing this salad is to mix it thoroughly when the potatoes are still hot. Traditional Creole-style potato salad is creamy, with the potatoes having an almost-mashed texture.

Yields 4 servings

4 large Idaho potatoes
6 tbsp. finely chopped onions
2 tbsp. finely chopped bell pepper
2 tbsp. finely chopped fresh parsley
2 cloves garlic, chopped

2 tbsp. dried mustard
1½ cups mayonnaise
2 stalks celery, chopped
Salt and pepper to taste

Boil potatoes until tender, about 20 minutes. Cool, peel, and cut into chunks.

In a large bowl, combine the potatoes with the onions, bell pepper, celery, parsley, and garlic.

In a separate bowl, whisk dried mustard into mayonnaise. Stir into potatoes. Season with salt and pepper and chill until ready to serve.

Audible and Edible Segregation

Drummer Barry Martyn has been an important figure in the international jazz music scene since his earliest performing days in post-war London. He arrived in New Orleans, the birthplace of jazz, in January 1961 as a kid of just eighteen.

I was fortunate to meet Barry through Peggy Scott Laborde when he appeared with us on an episode of *Steppin' Out,* the television show that Peggy has produced for more than a quarter of a century for New Orleans' PBS affiliate, WYES. I've done her food coverage for the better part of the last decade. Listening to Barry talk about his early days in New Orleans and the special relationship he shared with the legendary cook Buster Holmes, I couldn't wait to get him into the studio for a *Louisiana Eats!* interview.

Barry began by explaining why he came to New Orleans in the first place: "I came to learn about jazz. If you want to learn about bagpipes you go to Scotland, so I came to New Orleans to learn about jazz. It was great, but the big thing that I had never seen anything like before in my life was the segregation."

Barry pointed out that segregation didn't exist in England, "because when you were running down into those air-raid shelters, you couldn't care less who you were running down there with—a Chinaman, black people, Aborigines—it would not make any difference. No, there was nothing like that there."

In segregated New Orleans in the sixties, it was just as illegal for whites to eat in black restaurants as it was for blacks to eat in white establishments, a big problem for the only white musician playing with all-black bands. Barry pointed out, "It's like, us three in the studio here today—the engineer, you, and I—when we get through with this interview, we'll say, 'Well, let's go get a beer, a coffee . . .' You couldn't do that then. That was the bad part. Luckily, one of the biggest friends of the traditional jazz scene in those days was Buster Holmes, who had a restaurant on Orleans and Burgundy, and Buster, he was the nicest man I ever met in the United States."

Chef Susan Spicer knew Buster very well too. On a

Louisiana Eats! tribute show we did about Buster, Susan shared, "My first memories of Buster were when I was a teenager, acting like a hippie in the Quarter with my friends. I'd scrape together some change and have rice and gravy at his great soul-food restaurant in the French Quarter."

Later, as a young apprentice chef, Susan traveled several times to cook with him at the Jazz Fest in Nice, France. "Buster did his great red beans and rice but also smothered chicken, peach cobbler—I wasn't paying much attention at the time that I was doing this," she remembered. "I knew he was a famous guy and everything, but if it was now, I'd be constantly looking over my shoulder."

I asked what she thought made his red beans so special, and she answered, "I think he would stir some margarine in at the end to enrich it." We both agreed that it was more likely just the magic of his hand stirring those beans.

"Buster was really a special guy," Susan reminisced. "When I opened Bayona in 1990, one day Buster drove himself over to my restaurant in his station wagon. And he got out, and came in. He said, 'I just wanted to tell you congratulations and see how you were doing.' We sat down and I asked what I could make for him and he said he wanted a cup of tea and some ice cream. So I sat there and had tea and ice cream with Buster Holmes at Bayona. I was so touched that he made that trip over to see me. That was probably the last time I saw him."

Barry remembers first hearing about Buster from musician friends who'd once told him, "'We'll meet you at Buster's.' I said, 'Where is that?' They told me, 'Orleans and Burgundy.'"

Soon, Barry and Buster became close personal friends. He remembered, "The official title of it was Holmes Bar and Restaurant, and Buster wasn't a chef, he was a cook. He would always tell you that.

"Buster's name was Clarence Buster Holmes. I remember his wife's name was Blanche, and his girlfriend's name was Georgia Lee. Georgia Lee put a cleaver in Buster's head and cut him. He had to go to the hospital. Then, she vanished. And there was a lady there whose name was Muriel Charles, but everyone called her Bebe, and when I tell the story, people ask, 'Was she black or was she white?' Well, there were no white people in Buster's when I went in there. I was about the only white person anywhere around that area, but as the years went on they had all those white hippies that came in." I had to laugh at that, after the way Susan had described herself the same way—a "hippie."

Barry recalled what a great bargain it was to eat at Buster's, because in the early 1960s a plate of red beans and rice with hot sausage was thirty-five cents. "But even then, if you didn't have enough money, then Buster wouldn't care—he would give you the food anyway. He would say he knew times were tough. He'd say, 'Here, take this.' He was a friend to all musicians.

"The characters that would accumulate there, you wouldn't believe. There was a guy called Cleave and he would talk very softly. There was him, another guy called Levi, and one who sold the lottery. They were the usual clientele of Buster's. But then, all the musicians: Kid Sheik, Kid Howard, John Handy, Louis Nelson—all of them—Fred Minor, a banjo player, were there too.

"In fact, they used to say, if you had a job come in real quick, you go to Buster's and you could hire the men for it. There were always two or three trumpet players there, a couple of cord players, a bass player.

"When it came to ordering, you didn't go in there and expect a menu to order from, you just had to ask Buster, 'What you cooking today?' Stuffed pork chops with white beans, or whatever, he would always save some for the musicians because they were the poorest bunch, but generous. Musicians, when they had money, the drinks were on the house. Everybody drank. And the waitress, Bebe, she would walk around barefoot sometimes."

The way that Buster made it so easy to dance around the restaurant-segregation issue, combined with the delicious memories of his food, were the good part for Barry, but the segregation issue among the musicians themselves was a very difficult matter.

"I am white, but it would be easier for a white person to go to a colored—as they used to call them in those days—restaurant than it would vice versa. The white people, well, they had the upper hand; it was as simple as that, and not all of them relished that idea, not all of them subscribed to it, but most people seemed to because they were brought up with it," he remembered.

But it was still a crime. Barry was once arrested for recording with a black orchestra. That helped prompt him to join the Black Musicians' Union. When I asked about it, he laughed, "Yes, that's a tale—I didn't attach that much importance to it. I had to get into the union to make a recording."

After all, he continued, "If you have all that other nonsense in your mind then it might be different, but I never really cared what the law said. I kind of lived a life outside the law. I wouldn't come six thousand miles to be thwarted by some guy holding up his hands and saying, 'You can't do that.' So I joined the colored union, as they called it. I lived up over Dixieland Hall on Bourbon Street in those days, on the second floor over where the girl's legs swing out. That was all I could afford.

"They called me to the phone and it was a call from *Ebony* magazine. I don't know where they got my number from. They said, 'What a wonderful thing you have done,' and they wanted me to do an interview with them. I said, 'Well, I don't know;' it wasn't that wonderful to me; I didn't do it for the notoriety or anything. I had to get into the union. There were two, so I joined the one where I knew the most people. I told them I am not interested in all that.

"Then came another call that same night. It was a guy saying, 'This is the Klan.' He said, 'You had better get out of that such-and-such locale or we are going to raise your voice a couple of octaves.'" Barry laughed, "Well, you see, I can still sing bass.

"I told him, 'Well, boys, you come upstairs here. There is no light.' I was young and foolish then. It was single file on that stair, and they would have to come one by one, and I could pick them off like a turkey shoot." Barry spent that night anxiously sitting on the stairs with a shotgun across his lap, "like Clint Eastwood," he laughs now. No one ever showed up.

Returning to his happy memories of Buster, Barry mused, "I guess I thought he was a bit of an oddity. You ever seen a picture of him? Well he was big, I would say around 260 pounds, and he looked something like a Chinaman. But he had such a beautiful smile and you had the feeling he wanted to give you everything. He wanted nothing in return. There was no angle with him.

"I went back to England to play with my band in May of 1962 and we brought back some souvenir photographs for Buster. He tacked them up on the restaurant walls along with memorabilia from other musicians as well." Eventually, the walls became a gallery of the who's who of New Orleans jazz musicians.

Buster was always willing to bring food to help fuel recording sessions. There's a famous recording Barry did at a place called Hope's Hall that he remembers in particular. "It was pretty cold that day, and we had to keep the shutters up because of segregation. People would call the police, so we kept the shutters closed or we would all go to jail," he said. "When I came up before a judge one time, he said, 'Well, you can't come here, mixing cream with coffee. You understand me boy?' I said, 'Yes, sir, I certainly do.' I went right back doing what I was doing as soon as I got away from there.

"Buster brought over this whole big pot of food and cakes and dessert and he came in the back way. It was piping hot and he set it down and he said, 'I want you boys to have a good time here.' He sat there listening to the music and there was never any mention of money.

He did that about four or five times when we were making records.

"It was unbelievable. I can't explain the man. He didn't want anything from you. There was nothing—you couldn't buy him a drink because he owned the place. What was he going to do, charge you for two drinks? He would give you food if he could see you were hungry. He never asked for anything back. He never said, 'Why don't you bring me over to England and I will do some cooking?' He never said anything like that."

Buster Holmes' World Famous Red Beans and Rice

Here is the recipe that is purported to be Buster's original.

Yields 8 servings

1 lb. red beans
1 onion, chopped
½ green bell pepper, chopped
1 lb. smoked ham hock

2 cloves garlic, minced
Salt and pepper to taste
¼ cup margarine
Cooked rice, for serving

Pick through the beans to remove any rocks. Wash beans and cover with water.

Add onion, bell pepper, ham hock, and garlic. Cook over a low flame until tender, about 2 hours. Add salt, pepper, and margarine, then cook for 5 minutes more. Serve over rice with Louisiana hot sauce and buttered French bread.

Peach and Blueberry Cobbler

Here's my peach cobbler recipe, in Buster's honor. Susan Spicer told me that he always used canned peaches, but I prefer it with fresh peaches when they're in season. Usually, blueberries ripen around the same time, and I like to combine them.

Yields 8-10 servings

1½ cups flour
⅓ cup sugar, plus additional if needed
1 tbsp. baking powder
¼ tsp. salt
½ cup butter, cold, cut into tablespoons

¾ cup sour cream
8 cups cubed, unpeeled peaches (approximately 12-16 peaches, depending on size)
1 pt. blueberries

Combine flour, sugar, baking powder, and salt in a food processor. Pulse to combine. Add butter to the dry ingredients in the food processor. Pulse 7 or 8 times, until the mixture reaches a cornmeal consistency.

Put the flour mixture into a large mixing bowl and add the sour cream, gently pressing together until the dough is fully combined. Divide into 10 pieces and form the pieces into patties with a 2" diameter. Cover and reserve in the refrigerator.

Preheat oven to 350 degrees. Mix fruit together with additional sugar if needed in a 9" x 13" baking dish. Top with the 10 dough patties. Bake for 50 to 60 minutes or until fruit is tender and topping is golden brown.

Brewing on the Bayou

I took an instant liking to the gentleman with the graying beard I met when he poured my first LA-31 beer. It turned out the beer he was serving in the craft beer booth at the annual Louisiana Restaurant Association trade show was his own brew, made in the Cajun town of Arnaudville, Louisiana.

I soon learned that while he was growing up along the lazy waters of the Bayou Teche in Arnaudville, to Karlos Knott a beer meant a cold Bud guzzled to quench thirst.

Karlos stretched his wings by joining the US Army Calvary. Leaving behind his ancestral home, Knott, along with his young wife and baby, was stationed overseas in Germany.

These were exciting times for the young soldier. The Berlin Wall came down while he was there, opening up opportunities to cross the border and sample German brews that had not been available in the free world since before World War II. European beers opened Karlos' mind to flavors that he had never imagined. His time in the Army revealed a whole new gustatory world to the small-town boy, and he became fascinated with the way beer varieties paired with food.

Karlos' beer education continued stateside when, in the early 1990s, he was stationed at Fort Lewis, Washington. The Pacific Northwest was in the full swing of the new microbrewery movement. Karlos studied the various techniques of microbrewers there and began experimenting himself. Before too long, he was producing a pretty good *hefeweizen*, a German wheat beer not then available then in the US.

When Karlos retired from the Army, he returned to Arnaudville to his two Knott brothers, at long last reunited on the family's forty acres. The youngest brother, Dorsey, had worked in the Air Force as a purchasing agent, acquiring inventory-management skills. Byron had become an accomplished artist with a distinctive pop-art style, with works displayed in galleries and art shows throughout Louisiana. All three brothers built houses on their family's land, a heritage and a way of life they describe as "a family Utopia."

All that was missing was great beer. Using old-style European brewing techniques, Karlos began developing beers that would pair well with the unique flavors of the area's Cajun and Creole food. By 2009, the brothers decided to establish a brewery right there on Louisiana Highway 31 in their hometown of Arnaudville. Brother Byron caught the brewing bug from Karlos, and he regularly dreams up new beers, often using "non-traditional and, frankly, bizarre ingredients and techniques."

Karlos' twenty-eight-year-old son, Cory, wears many hats at the family's farmhouse brewery. In addition to brewing, washing kegs, and cleaning equipment, he incorporates his artistic talents into his work. Much like his uncle Byron, he works in a style they call zydeco pop. Cory silkscreens the brewery tee-shirts and paints and designs all of the LA-31 packaging, labels, and marketing materials. The brewery is filled with large canvases of Bayou Teche and Cajun-themed art.

The youngest Knott brother, Dorsey's, experiences as a contract specialist in the US Air Force, operations manager of a regional data-integration company, and the general manager of a food-distribution warehouse have uniquely prepared him for both sales and inventory management at the brewery.

Every Sunday during crawfish season, the Knott clan can be found boiling up a mess of mudbugs, trapped nearby in the family's crawfish pond. Extended family gathers in the brewery's outdoor communal kitchen, always with an ice chest of cold LA-31s nearby. Karlos claims, "We may be the only brewery in America that has our own crawfish pond. Most weekends during the season we boil the catch from my brothers, Byron and Dorsey. For us, boiling crawfish is not only a meal but an event. With every batch we boil, it's natural that Cajuns delight in the gathering of their family and friends. We can't ever get enough boiled crawfish; we dread the arrival of June when crawfish season is nearing its end."

In the spring of 2013, the Knott family was busy taste-testing a new brew, Saison d'écrevisses (crawfish-season ale), made specifically to pair well with spicy boiled crawfish. They brewed it as a Saison, a centuries-old Belgian style of farmhouse ale, crafted in limited quantities specifically for spring. Karlos told me, "In Belgium farmhouses, it's really considered the best beer of the year, and they drink it to celebrate the planting and the coming of springtime. For us, it helps to celebrate the springtime arrival of the crawfish."

What a story I heard over that first beer with Karlos Knott! I discovered that aside from the Knott brothers, Karlos' favorite collaborator is the Cajun band Lost Bayou Ramblers' lead musician, Louis Michot. Despite the almost twenty-year age difference, Karlos, fifty, and Louis, thirty-four, are great friends, always looking for ways to work together to protect and preserve the Cajun language and its culture.

Karlos and Louis had met over a beer as well. I heard that story the first time they sat down together in the WWNO studio for an interview. The Lost Bayou Ramblers had gotten LA-31 to donate beer for the studio recording sessions of their *Mammoth Waltz* album in 2012. During those recordings, when he heard the young Ramblers singing in Cajun French, Karlos got to thinking.

Karlos had not been allowed to learn the French of his heritage. When his parents were growing up in Acadiana, Karlos told me, "They wanted everyone to know English because it was the language of commerce, and they figured it would help the people get ahead down in our part of Louisiana. My parents were native French speakers who were publicly humiliated at school and not allowed to speak their native language. They, of course, did not want us to go through that, so they did not teach us French at all, because there was a stigma attached to it."

Hearing the Lost Bayou Ramblers, Karlos saw a way to help preserve the language of his heritage. "That's how Karlos got the idea to produce a CD with us that we called *En Français,* Louis told me. "Karlos came up with the idea to take really well-known classic rock tunes and put them into Cajun French, because people already knew at least some of the words in English. Songs like, 'You're No Good,' 'My Generation,' and 'Hey Joe.' So when you hear it in Cajun French, you can say, 'Well, I know what it is in English, so this teaches me how to say it in Cajun French.'"

The first *En Français* was such a success that they decided to produce a second album. Louis excitedly explained, "This time we had a whole new round of bands—amazing diversity—from the young Babineaux Sisters to Beau Soleil." Karlos added, "The nice thing about this CD is that it has more of a generational feel, because many of the bands had kids, their parents, their grandparents all in the studio together. It gave kind of a different groove to the whole thing."

Karlos refers to Louis as a "modern-day Thomas Jefferson." Not just a Cajun musician, this visionary, cultural conservationist is fighting on many fronts to preserve a way of life in what he fears could one day be "Bayou Perdu," or Lost Bayou, the name he chose for his Grammy-nominated band.

Louis' grandfather, Papa Lou, an accomplished musician in his own right, nurtured the traditional Cajun, agrarian lifestyle in Louis by letting him plant a small plot on his land in Pilette, Louisiana, near Lafayette, where they farmed together. They grew vegetables and picked wild blackberries and loquats to make the sweet, alcoholic beverage known as bounce.

Louis learned the delicious satisfaction of a harvest that reappears smothered, stewed, or fried on the family dinner table—but he'd never thought much about the seeds themselves until one day, while driving near Cypremort Point, he saw a sign that said "homegrown." His curiosity piqued, he stopped and knocked at the door.

An elderly woman answered and showed him the heirloom seedlings that she was selling for twenty-five cents per plant. She had mostly bell peppers and tomatoes for sale. Once planted in his home garden, Louis recognized the taste of his heritage in those heirlooms.

He began to actively seek out other Louisiana heirloom varieties, often speaking Cajun French with the men and women whose families had saved and replanted the seeds year after year on their land. Along the way, Louis discovered that "so much of the knowledge is tied up in the language." Again and again, he learned new words for growing techniques that did not have parallel words in English. For instance, a Cajun would say *boulé* to indicate that you grab a handful of dirt to make a hole for planting and then place the dirt back on top—a paragraph of instructions in a single word.

He obtained seeds for the longhorn and fathorn okras, which grew effortlessly in the steamy, hot climate. He found the rare Casse-Banane de Bresil bean and the exotically purple-striped green beans, called Zydeco Barré-Violet.

Louis gathered medicinal secrets as well as old wives tales while seed collecting. One of his favorites is the superstitious lore attached to the Mamou seed, also known as the coral bean because of its brilliant red color. For hundreds of years, Acadian French *traiteurs,* who combined prayer with herbal medicines, knew that a tea made from the seeds would relieve coughs and colds. Typical of the mystical *traiteur* style of medicine, it would only be concocted using an odd number of seeds, such as seven or eleven. The root of the Mamou plant was boiled, then the boiling liquid was sweetened into a syrup, historically available in pharmacies throughout Acadiana and said to have the same active ingredient as Robitussin cough syrup. Cajun women never drill a hole into Mamou seeds for stringing necklaces despite their bright, jewel-like appearance. Bayou legend claims that wearing a Mamou-seed necklace once caused the death of a young girl.

Following Hurricane Katrina, when many of these endangered seeds were lost due to salinized soils from flooded lands and wetlands loss, Louis began his own non-profit organization, the Cultural Research Institute of Acadiana. Its acronym, CRIA, means, "cry out" in Cajun French. CRIA's mission is to sustain the cultural and agricultural traditions of South Louisiana through preserving edible and medicinal seeds and knowledge and encouraging a traditional, sustainable lifestyle in an ecosystem increasingly endangered by natural and manmade disaster.

When he speaks of Louis' visionary work with CRIA, Karlos proudly points out that "each plant has a story."

That is what inspired him to include a CRIA heirloom garden on the Bayou Teche Brewery's property.

The entire crew at the brewery is devoted to creating the greenest, most sustainable operation possible—one that would improve the surrounding land and bayou and leave the smallest possible carbon footprint behind.

Beyond the garden, the land slopes gently down toward the bayou. Ten years ago, the bayou was a cesspool. Through the work of Blake Couvillion and his organization, Cajuns for Bayou Teche, the waterway is on its way back to its pristine origins. Tour de Teche has become an annual festival, bringing residents and visitors back to the bayou's banks.

Working with a professor from the University of California, Berkeley, Karlos arranged for the construction of a retention pond and marsh to process the brewery's wastewater. A ten-foot-deep retention pond slopes down to a shallow, one-and-a-half-foot-deep marsh with filtering cattails growing in it. By the time the water reaches the Teche, it's almost drinkable. One of the great treats of Karlos' day is witnessing the array of wildlife—birds, deer, and more—that stops at the retention pond to have a little sip of water or hunt an unsuspecting crawfish.

Whether they're visiting over cups of the thick, black café noir that's so beloved by generations of Cajuns or testing the latest batch of brew, Karlos and Louis agree about the generations-old Cajun country adage: "Ça, c'est bon!" Life on the Teche is good indeed!

Merde sur un Bardeau

During his Army career, Karlos became well acquainted with the daily breakfast of soldiers, "shit on a shingle." Back in Acadiana, he now makes a delicious version with crawfish. The French name certainly adds some much-needed panache.

Yields 4 servings

¼ cup butter
1 small yellow onion, diced
6 oz. tasso, diced
1 clove of garlic, minced
1 8-oz. bottle clam juice

½ pt. whipping cream
Salt, black pepper, and cayenne pepper to taste
½ lb. crawfish tails
4 green onions, chopped
Fresh parsley, minced, for garnish

Melt the butter in a large sauté pan and add the onion and tasso. Sauté until the onion is soft and the tasso is browned and somewhat crispy. Add the garlic and sauté until aromatic, around 1 minute. Pour in the claim juice and cook over medium heat until reduced by half. Add the cream and salt, black pepper, and cayenne pepper, and continue cooking until thick and creamy, reducing by about half. Stir in the crawfish and green onions and cook for another 5 minutes. Adjust seasonings as needed. Garnish with parsley and serve over buttered toast or open-faced biscuits.

Zydeco Salé

The Cajun music term "zydeco" is said to originally come from the French phrase "Les haricots ne sont pas salés," "the snap beans are not salty." When spoken in the Cajun French vernacular, which has is largely an oral language, it sounds like "leh-ZY-dee-co sohn pah salEH," in bayou country often meaning, "I have no spicy news for you." It is not surprising that this is Louis' favorite way to cook the string beans he grows at home.

Yields 6 servings

2 tbsp. oil
1 cup tasso, diced
2 tbsp. butter

2 lbs. young green beans
½ cup water
Salt and pepper to taste

Heat the oil in a heavy skillet. Add the tasso and brown well. Add the butter and green beans. Cook, uncovered, over medium heat for 20 minutes, stirring frequently. Add water, ¼ cup at a time, scraping up any bits sticking to the bottom of the pan. When beans are tender, season with salt and pepper and serve.

Cajun Shrimp Stew

In the very Catholic South Louisiana of Karlos' youth, shrimp stew was served nearly every Friday. Here's the original family recipe, passed down through generations.

Yields 4 servings

⅓ cup flour
⅓ cup vegetable oil
1 medium onion, chopped
½ bell pepper, chopped
1 stalk celery, chopped
2 cloves garlic, minced

2 cups water, plus additional if needed
2 tsp. seafood stock base
Salt, black pepper, and cayenne pepper to taste
1 lb. shrimp, cleaned and peeled
½ cup sliced green onions
Cooked rice, for serving

Make a roux by stirring together the flour and oil in a cast-iron skillet over medium heat until it is the color of chocolate milk. Add the onion, followed by the bell pepper and celery. Cook until softened, about 10 minutes, then add the garlic.

Scrape the roux and vegetables into a stockpot, add the water and the seafood stock base, and bring to a boil, stirring until well combined and adding additional water as needed if gravy becomes too dry. Reduce the heat and add salt, black pepper, and cayenne pepper to taste and simmer uncovered for another half hour. Stir in the shrimp and green onions and cook until shrimp are pink, about 3 additional minutes. Adjust seasonings as needed. Serve over rice.

Cornbread Supper

In the old agrarian days of Acadiana, the midday meal was the largest of the day. In the evening, most people would have a light supper of cornbread and milk. Today, Karlos maintains that tradition, but augments the cornbread with meat and vegetables for a more filling evening meal.

Yields 4 servings

1 12" skillet of cornbread
1 onion, chopped
2 stalks celery, chopped
1 bell pepper, chopped
½ cup chopped green onions
1 lb. smoked sausage, diced (feel free to substitute or combine with andouille, tasso, ham, or shrimp, as desired)

¼ cup butter
3 cloves garlic, minced
1 tbsp. chopped fresh thyme
Salt, black pepper, and cayenne pepper to taste
⅓ cup chopped flat-leaf parsley
3 cups chicken stock, plus additional if needed

Crumble the cornbread in a large bowl.

In a skillet, sauté the onion, celery, bell pepper, green onions, and sausage in the butter until onions are soft, about 10 minutes. Add the garlic and thyme.

Preheat oven to 350 degrees. Pour sausage mixture into the bowl with the cornbread and add salt, black pepper, and cayenne pepper to taste, parsley, and chicken stock. Stir to mix and add more chicken stock only if the mixture is not moist enough. Adjust seasonings if needed.

Spread the cornbread mixture in an 11" x 7" lightly greased baking dish and cover with foil. Bake for about 20 minutes, remove the foil, and bake uncovered for an additional 15 minutes.

A Streetcar Ride with a Poor Boy

A professor of history at the University of New Orleans, Michael Mizell-Nelson's many obsessions include both streetcars and poor boys, two essential New Orleans subjects. The St. Charles Avenue streetcar line began running in 1835 and is today the oldest continuously operating streetcar line in the world. The poor boy, meanwhile, didn't show up in New Orleans with that name until 1929. Still, streetcars and poor boy sandwiches are inextricably linked in the city's history books and cultural memory.

Michael helped found the Oak Street Po-Boy Festival in 2007 in conjunction with members of the Leidenheimer Baking Company family. He also produced the documentary film *Streetcar Stories*. His knowledge about the history and lore of the New Orleans streetcars and the role they played in our food heritage would fascinate our *Louisiana Eats!* audience.

My sound engineer, Thomas Walsh, and I met Michael at the stop closest to the St. Charles streetcar barn, at Willow Street and Carrollton Avenue. We recorded the conversation while riding the original St. Charles car back and forth on the entire route. An old-fashioned atmosphere endures on New Orleans' streetcars despite the fact that, even today, they are an important part of the city's transportation system— many New Orleanians ride them daily to and from work and school. At one point, when we reached the end of the line at Carrollton and Claiborne Avenues, we heard a man's voice ring out, "Ice cold water! Fresh pecan pralines!" adding an old-time texture to our conversation.

As we rode the swaying car, Michael told us about the history of this city icon: "Until the mid-twentieth century, streetcars were actually used for food delivery. The lady of the house would place an order with a grocer or restaurant, asking to have the goods delivered to a certain stop on the line. The streetcar driver would hand off the food at the designated stop, often receiving a pack of gum or cigarettes as a tip."

He told me that the streetcar also gave rise to "impromptu markets that often sprung up at the end of the line or at other stops, with backyard farmers selling fruit and vegetables grown nearby. On Fridays in particular, men would hop on the car near the Riverbend and walk the aisles holding just-caught river catfish by the gills, offering them for sale to the riders on their way home from work."

Although vendors frequently transported shrimp and live crabs by streetcar, they were prohibited from carrying live crawfish, as it was believed they might carry disease. However, sometimes passengers would hear a quiet "moo" coming from under the "beauty seats," the long benches that run parallel to the aisle in the front and back of the car. Drivers on the St. Claude line sometimes purchased calves from a farm on the rural route through St. Bernard Parish and stashed them underneath the streetcar's benches until they could be delivered to the neighborhood butcher.

Motormen and conductors worked long hours, so management sanctioned regular breaks. Compagno's Restaurant at Fern Street and St. Charles Avenue was a regular stop for the drivers. When the car stopped, it would trip an automatic three-minute timer, the maximum break time allowed. Calling out an order for a cold ham and cheese poor boy, the streetcar drivers and motormen would avail themselves of the restroom and then grab cold sandwiches on their way back out in order to consume them on the route.

Michael said, "In the careful way that life was meted out back then, if they wanted a hot sandwich, it could be ordered at Compagno's and then fifty-six or fifty-seven minutes later, when they made the round-trip, it would be ready for them, and that too would be eaten on the streetcar." Family members of some of the workers remember delivering the evening meal to dad and dining along with him as they rode the streetcar together.

To honor these intertwined traditions, we crafted an entire *Louisiana Eats!* episode dedicated to French bread and the sandwich it inspired, with Michael's streetcar stories combined with an interview with third-generation New Orleans French-bread baker John Gendusa.

I have known John Gendusa since the earliest days of Slow Food New Orleans. John Gendusa welcomed our chapter into his Gentilly bakery to show us just how one of those magic poor boy loaves are made.

When John and I sat down for the studio interview, he began by laughing and pointing out, "It's funny that the Italians are the French bread specialists here. We call it French bread, but my father was from Italy. We have bakers from Germany and all over but we don't have any real French men in New Orleans who make our style of French bread . . . It is a different and unique type of bread only found in here. It was made from the various people who came together and got this loaf together."

When talking about the poor boy sandwich, John said, "It's very airy. When you put meat or seafood on it, you can taste what you put on it instead of just having a lot of heavy doughy bread. It's very nice for a sandwich."

The origin of the poor boy sandwich is a well-documented New Orleans legend. It traces back to John's grandfather, the first John Gendusa, and brothers Benny and Clovis Martin, former streetcar conductors operating a small restaurant and bar across from the French Market. It was the summer of 1929, and a violent streetcar strike had erupted.

The conductors and motormen were protesting for a better living wage. As the summer wore on, the striking men were having a hard time making ends meet and especially feeding themselves and their families. So, the Martins posted notices all over town saying, "As long as the strike lasts, those poor boys will have a free meal at Martin Brothers Grocery." Benny and Clovis sat down with John Gendusa and, together, they sketched out the length of a sandwich that stretched approximately a yard long and could provide a meal to the strikers and their families. Previously, these sandwiches were known as "loaves", but by the early 1930s, as Michael Mizell-Nelson documents, the new name "poor boys" began to appear on New Orleans restaurant menus.

John Gendusa had already had a hand in creating the unique shape of the loaf. As his grandson remembers, "They were having problems because the real French bread, it's fat in the middle and pointed on the ends. So, if you got the skinny end of the sandwich, you didn't get much of a sandwich and they would get complaints.

"When my grandfather was a child back in Sicily, he used to go stay around the bakeries there and that's why he'd wanted to become a baker. He remembered back in Italy they made long, straight loaves with blunt instead of pointy ends. He made some for the Martins. They tried it and it turned out great."

I asked John why he thought that New Orleans French bread could only be made in New Orleans. "I don't know really," he answered. "It could be several factors. One could be the water. One could be the air. Also, it could be the bakeries being here for so long, in the same places that they've always been in. The yeast that builds itself up in the building can give the bread a specific flavor . . . . When I left my old bakery and came to the new bakery, I took some old dough with me and put it all around the building so I could get the yeast into the new building."

But then he added, "I consider the New Orleans water to be one of the biggest factors . . . The water definitely has a big effect on the taste of the bread and the outcome of the bread being light and fluffy."

John also told me that when he was growing up, his father had shared a story with him: "My father had two top-notch bakers who left and went to Baton Rouge. They were going to make New Orleans French bread but they never could do it. They tried and tried. They came back and talked to my father and never could find out what was wrong and how to make a loaf of New Orleans French bread in Baton Rouge. My father tried to help them out but, with everything they did, nothing came to pass to make a good loaf of New Orleans French bread in Baton Rouge." That is a pretty amazing tale, considering that Baton Rouge is only eighty miles away from the birthplace of the poor boy loaf.

Knowing how precious the food heritage of the Gendusa family is, I asked John about the future. He answered, "The future is my son. He's been in for ten years now and he's just about getting ready to learn how to make a loaf of French bread . . . Daddy still has to show him a few things, but he's getting down to the point where he can make a very good loaf of bread."

John told me that over the years he's had all sorts of people work for him at the bakery. He laughed and said, "We had a fellow by the name of Kermit Ruffins who worked for us." Kermit Ruffins is now one of New Orleans' most famous twenty-first-century jazz musicians.

John reminisced, "He was a bread driver for me. He and a friend of his left and went to Atlanta and they were blowing their horns there. They stayed quite a few years. I saw Kermit again recently and we talked about the old times, how he'd miss a day's work because he'd blown his horn too late in the morning and couldn't make it in to work."

I found John's story about Kermit particularly striking when my next-door neighbor, Jennifer Eagan, forwarded to me an e-mail her dad had sent his family describing a special moment he'd shared with a hot loaf of French bread.

Jennifer's father, Gerry Bodet, was among the earliest faculty members at the University of New Orleans, joining the history department in 1961, where he continues to teach today as an emeritus professor.

"Pops," as he's known to his grandchildren, has lived all of his seventy-plus years in New Orleans neighborhoods: Broadmoor, Uptown, Gentilly, and, now, Mid-City, within walking distance of Jazz Fest.

Along for the ride has been Janice, Jennifer's mother and Gerry's wife of fifty-one years, and their clan of seven children. Naturally, French bread was a staple in the Bodet household all those years.

This is the e-mail that Gerry wrote to his family:

Hello All:

Kermit Ruffins has a song in which he asks, "What is New Orleans," and answers with stories about food. I had such a food experience today on my way home. My destination was Johnny's Hardware, in Gentilly, at "Meraboo and St. Ant-ny."But it happens that Johnny's is next door to John Gendusa's French Bread Bakery. As I walked back to the car I had an irresistible urge to get a loaf. It was a cold March day, and standing outside in forty-five degrees, the warm smell of freshly baked French bread wafted over me, an aroma like no other. "Whadaya need?" came the question. "A long loaf, or any loaf." "Dollah fifty."

Is there any place on this planet where one can buy a piece of heaven for a dollar and fifty cents? By the time I reached home on the bayou the loaf was half gone and the front seat littered with crumbs. And, to give one answer to Kermit's question, *that* is New Orleans.

Love,
Dad/Pops

How could anyone argue the position that the esteemed history professor takes on New Orleans and its relationship with French bread? The poor boy has been the original fast-food meal in the Crescent City for more than a century. What a different place the city would have been—would be—without it! It's a place I hope we never have to know.

Roast Beef Poor Boy

My favorite roast beef poor boy is the dripping, delicious version served at Parkway Bakery. They serve hundreds of pounds of this fork-tender, fabulous roast beef every week on crispy, hot French bread. With some advice from Jay Nix, Parkway's owner, here is a version scaled down for your home kitchen.

Yields 6-8 poor boy sandwiches

1 3-4-lb. beef chuck roast
Salt and pepper to taste
3 garlic cloves
1 medium onion, cut into large chunks
2 tbsp. flat-leaf parsley
3 tbsp. vegetable oil
1 qt. beef stock

2 loaves poor boy bread
½ cup mayonnaise, for serving
1 head iceberg lettuce, shredded, for serving
3-4 thinly sliced tomatoes, for serving
1 16-oz. jar sliced dill pickles, for serving
Hot sauce to taste

Season the roast with salt and pepper.

With the food processor running, drop in the garlic cloves one at a time to finely chop them. Add the onion and the parsley to the food processor and chop, pulsing continuously until minced.

Preheat oven to 275 degrees. Heat the oil in a heavy, 5-quart Dutch oven. Brown the beef on all sides, then remove meat and reserve. Add onion mixture and sauté over medium heat until the onions are lightly browned, about 7 minutes. Add the stock and return the roast to the pot. Place two pieces of aluminum foil crosswise on the surface of the roast and gravy to give an extra seal to the pot. Put the lid on the pot and place in the oven for 6 to 8 hours.

Once done cooking and meat is tender, remove the roast from the oven and allow to cool. Thinly slice and shred the roast. Return to the liquid and reheat.

Lightly toast the French bread until crispy. Slice in half and liberally spread with mayonnaise. Assemble the poor boys by layering on the roast and gravy, topped with lettuce, tomatoes, and dill pickles. Season with hot sauce to taste and serve hot.

Savory Pain Perdu

Pain perdu (lost bread) is a centuries-old French breakfast tradition that has been a New Orleans staple since its earliest days. I love to serve this savory twist for brunch or lunch.

Yields 4 servings

8 1½"-thick slices of French bread,
8 oz. herbed soft cheese (goat, farmer's, or seasoned cream cheese), divided into 8 pieces
1½ cups milk
6 eggs
1 tbsp. hot sauce, or to taste
¼ cup butter
Chutney or pickled vegetable relish, for serving

Cut a pocket from the side of each piece of French bread into the center. Insert one piece of cheese into each slice of bread.

Whisk together the milk, eggs, and hot sauce. Briefly soak each piece of stuffed bread in the milk mixture.

Melt the butter in a 10" skillet, and, when large bubbles foam, add the French bread pieces. Cook for about 3 minutes per side or until lightly browned. Serve with chutney or a pickled vegetable relish.

Meat Dressing

This recipe is adapted from my memories of my great-grandmother's meat dressing. Meat dressing was a staple of Mamman's Thanksgiving dinner table. As I worked to try to replicate this treasured taste memory, I discovered the secret was New Orleans French bread. Because of its airy lightness, simply softening stale French bread with a little water before mixing it into any stuffing recipe adds an indefinable texture and taste that, like the bread itself, cannot be replicated with anything else.

Yields 10-12 servings

3 lbs. ground beef
1 onion, chopped
3 stalks celery, chopped
1 bell pepper, chopped
3 cups stale French bread
1 cup water, plus additional if needed

¼ cup Lea & Perrins Worcestershire sauce
6-8 green onions, thinly sliced
2 cloves garlic, minced
¼ cup chopped fresh parsley
Salt and black pepper to taste

Brown the ground beef in a heavy Dutch oven. Add the onion, celery, and bell pepper and sauté until onions are translucent. Remove from heat.

Preheat oven to 325 degrees. In a large bowl, mix together French bread and water, adding more water if needed until bread is very damp. Add ground beef mixture, the Worcestershire sauce, green onions, garlic, parsley, salt, and pepper. Pour into an ungreased baking dish. Bake for 25 or 35 minutes until heated through and browned on top.

The Song of the Sausage Man

When I asked Vance Vaucresson to say a few words before the interview began so that the studio engineer could set the sound levels on his microphone, we got a song:

> I got dat hot sausage, you got dem buns.
> Let's put 'em together and have some fun.
> I'll bring that mayonnaise, that Creole mustard too.
> Don't forget that cheese!
> I got that hot sausage, then let's make lovin' too!

That was little surprise, coming from the fourth-generation sausage maker who remembers his dad always saying that Vaucresson sausage tasted so good because "We make it with love."

I've always been a fan of that delicious sausage and never fail to save room for a spicy Vaucresson hot sausage poor boy at Jazz Fest, but I didn't really get to know the man behind the sausage until a rallying cry resounded in the New Orleans food world a few months after Hurricane Katrina.

In *GQ Magazine*'s November 2006 issue, food writer Alan Richman made a now-infamous remark doubting the existence of Creoles. "I have never met one and suspect they are a faerie folk, like leprechauns, rather than an indigenous race," he wrote. New Orleanians became incensed, and writer Kim Severson fired back with a December 2006 piece in the *New York Times* entitled "'Faerie Folk' Strike Back with Fritters."

Kim and I became fast friends during the extensive time she spent reporting in New Orleans following Katrina. After reading Mr. Richman's insulting article, she asked whether I could assemble some of the purported "faeries" in my home for an interview and photo shoot. I knew of Vance and invited him on a whim.

After a long morning of discussing the Creole heritage of our city accompanied by calas and café au lait styled for the camera (and then promptly devoured), Vance pronounced me his new Creole "cousine." He only required that I drop the 'r' in my last name and add a French accent aigu over the e. "As Poppy Tooké," he said, I would surely pass.

A look into the branches of the Vaucresson family tree made that a real possibility. As Vance described it during his *Louisiana Eats!* interview, "Creole New Orleans—especially Creoles of color—when you go to trace your background, you start reaching these branches where we've got French, Polish Jewish, Cherokee, East Indian, Spanish. It just goes and goes. We came to find out my great-grandfather, Lovinsky Vaucresson, was a French-Polish Jew from the Alsace-Lorraine region of France. He was married to a French woman of color named Odile Gaillard, and eventually they made their way to New Orleans and settled.

"Knowing there's a distinctive Polish as well as Jewish heritage, it makes us not only appreciate and love the fact that we are a black people in this society, but it really makes you appreciate the other branches of your background, especially being a sausage maker. Polish are known for doing very well with meats, so maybe that helped in our background," Vance mused.

Lovinsky Vaucresson was a butcher known for his sausage. His son, Robert Lovinsky Vaucresson, was born with a great entrepreneurial spirit. He also became a butcher and had a stall in the St. Bernard Market that later became Circle Food Store. Eventually, he opened his own meat market on the corner of N. Johnson Street and St. Bernard Avenue in the Seventh Ward.

Robert Vaucresson only had one son, but not for lack of trying. The hard-working butcher married three times. His first marriage produced three daughters. There were no children with the second union. But, when he married for the third time, his first child was Sonny Vaucresson, his only son.

Vance said, "My aunts told me there was nothing my dad could do wrong. He walked on water in that house. He was a free spirit." As a young man, Sonny served in the military and was stationed in France. During his time there, he discovered a small town about fourteen miles outside of Paris called Vaucresson. When he came home with photos of the town that bore the family name, Vance said, "it became our family's Mecca."

Sonny attended Xavier University, "but didn't finish," Vance said. "My grandfather passed, so Dad had to stop school and take over the business. But he didn't want to just be a butcher and do the meat market, so he got together with some of his older sisters' husbands and they got into the liquor store business." Sonny also had a cigarette machine company and invested in real estate.

Sonny's most notable investment occurred when he and his friend Larry Borenstein, a successful businessman with a lot of property in the French Quarter, decided to open a Creole restaurant at 624 Bourbon Street, Vaucresson's Café Creole, which operated from 1965 to 1974. Vance said, "At that time in the Quarter, there wasn't any restaurant serving dishes from the tradition of the Creoles of color in the city: grits and grillades, red beans and rice with chaurice sausage on the side." Perhaps the most remarkable thing about Sonny's restaurant was that it was the first business to be owned by a person of color on Bourbon Street since Reconstruction.

Vance described his father as "very fair skinned. He had sky-blue eyes and just did not look like a person of color. Even though he never denounced that he was a man of color, he just didn't look it. So, a lot of people, when they got to know Sonny, they knew Sonny—not so much Sonny with the label of being a black man or a Creole."

He continued, "A lot of major players in the Quarter—like the Carnot family, the Caracci family, the Cahns—they all got to know my dad and did business with him.

So, when the idea came up to open a restaurant with Larry Borenstein, all the powers that be got together and blessed this particular union. They said, 'Oh if it's Sonny, then that's okay.'"

But in the turbulent racial climate of the mid-sixties, rumors about the new restaurant began to circulate. Vance said, "There was a meeting of the Bourbon Street Merchants Association where one of the hushed topics was that word on the street was . . ."

Vance paused, and, before continuing the story, he said, "I'm not going to use the ugly word that they used then, but they said, 'One of those N-word people was coming onto Bourbon Street.' The discussion turned to how it was going to bring the property values down and all these people were going to start coming into these establishments and really mess up Bourbon Street.

"One of the white gentlemen who my dad had known for years in the Quarter sat down with Dad and Larry and said, 'I'm just so upset that this guy is coming—I just can't believe this.' And he looks around the room, looking for the guy.

"Larry Borenstein says, 'Look, I know the guy. I'm going to introduce you to him.' The white guy, he says, 'Oh, please, I need to know who he is. That way, I can keep my eye on him.' Then Larry continued, 'Well, you know Sonny.' And the guy says, 'Yeah, of course I know Sonny. I just shook hands with him and gave him a hug.' Larry answered, 'Well, he's the new N-word on Bourbon Street.' My dad told me, 'The guy turned pale white, began to sweat, and got up from the table and left.' So, without further ado, Larry and Sonny opened their restaurant on Bourbon Street."

According to Vaucresson family history, it was there, Vaucresson's Café Creole, that the seed of the New Orleans Jazz and Heritage Festival was planted. George Wein, who had founded the Newport Jazz Festival in 1954, and Larry Borenstein were catching up at the restaurant. Larry had recently brought Alan Jaffe to New Orleans to run Preservation Hall, which Borenstein had founded. Alan Jaffe was at the table, and so was Sonny.

George was telling his friends about the success of the most recent Newport Jazz Festival, and the talk turned to why the birthplace of jazz didn't have something that explains and celebrates the essence of what and who we are. As the brainstorming continued, the element of food quickly entered into the mix. Someone suggested, "Sonny could bring food from the restaurant," Vance told me.

When the very first New Orleans Jazz Fest was held at Congo Square in 1970, organizers asked Sonny to make some poor boys and bring them over to sell. Vance was there too. He was less than a year old, but family legend includes the story of Vance being carried over to the square in his mother's arms.

Vance described how his dad would wrap the sausage poor boys "up in foil at the restaurant and bring them out to the booth. Dad used to say at that first festival there were more musicians walking around than patrons, but there was an air at that first festival. The people there knew this was something special."

Now, thousands of Vaucresson Sausage poor boys are sold at the festival each year, but, Vance said, "For the first few years, it was very lean, and we were lucky to break even—but the family continued to participate because Sonny felt a little bit of ownership in the fest because of how it came about and how he was there at the beginning.

"The second festival was held on the fairgrounds, and there were just five or six vendors. We used it as a way for us to promote our product. Eventually, the booth would provide a little bit of extra money during the year."

As it grew, Vance remembers his mom saying, "Oh, I pay your tuition with that festival money. That festival money always came in handy."

When the country's food critics began to attend and take notice, things really exploded with the festival's food. Vance recalled, "In 1976, the festival held what was called the 'Food Olympics.' Mimi Sheraton from the *New York Times* came down to judge the food, and she proclaimed Vaucresson Hot Sausage as the best food at the fest."

Looking back at growing up as a Vaucresson, Vance said, "When you have a family-owned business, you come up in the business all your life. Me and my brothers all started working in the business when we were eight to ten years old, doing whatever little jobs we could. The challenge for us was to decide when we got older who was going to be the next generation in the business."

Vance was the youngest of Sonny's three sons. After high school, he went to Morehouse College in Atlanta, and when he was a senior, his dad came to see him. Sonny said, "Son, you know I've got this business and I really need some help. I know you're graduating, and I really wish you'd come back and work in the family business." Vance already had a job lined up with Kraft General Foods after graduation, but promised Sonny he'd give it some thought. He decided to honor his father's request and return home to New Orleans and the Vaucresson Sausage business.

Reflecting on that decision today, Vance said, "In the black community, having a generational business that keeps going and going—it's rare. I made the decision to come back home. Working with my dad was like being baptized by fire, because if we didn't argue or fuss every day, I thought something was wrong. I'd learned all this business theory in college, but Dad had his many years of hands-on learning and the trials and tribulations that came with that.

"But the seven years I worked side by side with Dad until he had his heart attack were some of the greatest years I had, because I realized after he left that having those seven years of arguing with him every day, he was training me. Toughening my skin. He was getting me ready."

Sonny died in 1998 at the age of sixty-seven. Vance remembered, "It was a Sunday and I was working the Alligator Fest in Boutte. Dad and I had recently made some great strides in the business, striking a deal with the Orleans Parish school system. We were going to distribute to them ourselves and had done all this planning to deliver to 115 schools in one day. We had trucks we had rented and people we had added on and had tens of thousands of pounds of product in our freezer and coolers. Our first delivery was going to be that Monday morning and we were so proud of ourselves.

"That Sunday was All Saints Day, and so, being a good Creole Catholic, he went with my mother and his sister to visit all the relatives in the cemetery." But Sonny didn't look right. "He started to get a little peaked and flushed in the face," Vance continued. "My aunt forced him to go to the hospital. My dad was deathly afraid of the doctor.

"He had his heart attack right outside of Ocshner Hospital and they carried him into the emergency room. They called me on a pay phone at the festival and said he'd had a heart attack. I went to the hospital, and I didn't get a chance to see him. He died on the table.

"But I had a feeling at the pay phone. I knew. I just had this feeling that didn't think he was going to recover from this. So I just knew: okay, it's yours now, and you're going to have to step up.

"That night, I spent the night with Mom at the home. It was just she and I lying on the bed and we were looking up at the ceiling talking, trying to figure out what to do. She says, 'What are you going to do?' I said, 'Well, knowing my dad, I gotta get up at five and go start loading those trucks. We worked so hard on this contract I can't let this stop.'

"So there wasn't any mourning time for me. I walked in and all the people were there, waiting for me, and I said, 'Sonny's not coming. He passed yesterday. But knowing him, we got to keep this going.' I opened up the doors of the factory, and then I broke down and cried for about five minutes, wiped my tears. We started loading those trucks, and the rest is history."

With the determination of a proud, fourth-generation sausage maker, Vance forged ahead when Hurricane Katrina wiped out the Vaucresson family's factory as well as their homes. He found a facility where he could produce the famous family sausage and was on the fairgrounds on opening day of Jazz Fest in 2006, just eight months after the hurricane.

"You don't hear much about sausage people being singers, but we all sing," Vance said. Acclaimed New Orleans jazz singers Lillian and John Boutté are first cousins who have been known to enlist him for back-up vocals.

"My cousin John called up one day and said, 'Man, you know, Vance, I need you to come over here and do a little background singing for me. I'm singing this album, *Jambalaya,* and I really need you to come and put a little background in it. Now, you know, I don't have any money to pay you so we gonna put it on that family love we have.' You get that free labor from your people," Vance said.

Vance is proud that when one of the songs on *Jambalaya* got picked up as the theme for HBO's series *Treme,* John Boutté's fame increased appreciably—even though Vance claims that you can hardly tell which back-up voice is his.

"Eventually, I'm going to remarket myself as the singing sausage man," he continued. "Every year at the festival, when John sings in the Jazz Tent, I leave my booth and go sing background with him. But I told him, the only thing I ask is I need to keep my Vaucresson Sausage tee-shirt on, so I can get that little extra publicity to help the crowd find their way over to the booth for that after-concert treat."

When you come to the New Orleans Jazz and Heritage Festival, don't miss the singing sausage man. And here's fair warning: one Vaucresson Sausage poor boy just might not be enough.

Hot Sausage Balls

Hot Sausage Balls are a Vaucresson family favorite. This very easy recipe comes from the kitchen of Vance and his wife, Julie.

Yields about 4 dozen balls

1 lb. spicy bulk pork sausage
8 oz. sharp Cheddar cheese, grated, room
  temperature

3 cups biscuit mix

Preheat the oven to 350 degrees.

Place the sausage, cheese, and biscuit mix in a large bowl and mix by hand until well combined. Shape into 1" balls. Arrange the balls about 1" apart on ungreased baking sheets. Bake until cooked through and well browned, about 12 to 15 minutes. Serve hot.

Originally published in The Southern Foodways Alliance Community Cookbook.

Crawfish-Stuffed Bell Peppers

Aside from the famous hot sausage, the Vaucressons also make a crawfish sausage that also is served in a poor boy at Jazz Fest every year. Here's my favorite thing to do with it instead!

Yields 6 servings

3 large bell peppers
8 tbsp. butter, divided
1 stalk celery, finely chopped
2 cloves garlic, minced
3 green onions, finely chopped

3 tbsp. minced flat-leaf parsley
1 lb. Vaucresson Crawfish Sausage
½ loaf stale French bread
¼ cup plain breadcrumbs
Salt and pepper to taste

Preheat oven to 350 degrees.

Cut the crowns from the bell peppers, finely chop, and set aside.

Split the body of the pepper in half and blanche in boiling water for 2 minutes. Remove from water and set aside.

Melt 6 tbsp. butter in a 10" skillet. Add the chopped bell pepper crowns, celery, garlic, green onions, and parsley, and cook over medium-low heat for 5 minutes.

Remove the crawfish sausage from the casing and crumble into the skillet, mixing well. Dampen the French bread with water until just moist. Add to the skillet and stir well. Season with salt and pepper to taste, then stuff mixture into bell pepper halves. Top with breadcrumbs and dot with remaining 2 tbsp. butter. Bake for 25 to 30 minutes until browned and heated through.

The Living Soil

Rice is a staple of Louisiana's diet. As early as 1718, Bienville's French colonists began cultivating the grain in low-lying areas adjoining the Mississippi River. But it wasn't until the railroad began running through the prairies of southwest Louisiana that major commercial production began. By 1892, two hundred million pounds of rice traveled annually by rail to New Orleans to be milled. At the same time, mechanically polished white rice became the standard on every table, despite the fact that most of the nutrition is found in the outer bran, which gives milled rice its light brown color.

Third-generation rice farmer Kurt Unkel is changing the way Louisianians eat rice with his Cajun Grain, a brown jasmine rice that he mills by hand before packing and delivering it to clamoring customers at the farmers markets of south Louisiana.

I met Kurt when he began selling his product at the Crescent City Farmers Market. The flavor of his rice quite simply blew my socks off. I'll confess that, unlike most Louisiana eaters, I prefer my rice with butter instead of gravy. But to me, Kurt's Cajun Grain stood in a category of its own. Much to my surprise, I loved eating it with just a little salt. The delicious flavor and popularity of Cajun Grain made Kurt an obvious choice for a *Louisiana Eats!* interview.

Fifteen years ago, Kurt and his brother, Hine, maintained two thousand acres of rice fields on their family farm near Kinder, Louisiana. Today, Kurt farms only twenty acres but is fully involved in every step of production, from harvest through direct sale to happy eaters. Each bag of rice is hand-stamped with the milling date. Kurt says that this is important because rice loses its nutritional value within six months of milling. (Storing the rice in your home freezer can slow the loss.)

My interview with Kurt took place on a busy Saturday at the Crescent City Farmers Market on Magazine Street in downtown New Orleans. Despite the three-plus hours he'd traveled that morning before the opening bell had rung at the market, Kurt was amazingly invigorated by the shoppers who quickly lined up to buy his unique product.

We stepped around the back of fellow farmer Timmy Perilloux's vegetable-laden truck, trying to find a place where the crowd's noise would be slightly muffled. I began by asking him what makes his rice so special. "I think it's just the soil, working with the soil. It's building the nutrients back in the soil. The whole trick is getting a living soil, and everything starts there." Kurt continued, "I didn't realize it years back, but I had a dead soil. I'd actually probably never seen a live soil. It smells good. It's fluffy. When you move it, you see little insects and animals and earth and everything just running round all over the place—and every time you look in it, you'll see new insects you've never seen before. You can just dig. It always looks like it's just been plowed. When you move your cover crop it's just loose and fluffy."

Eyes sparkling with excitement, he described his revelation. "The biggest thing is that the oxygen is in the soil. It's getting the air. It's getting the carbon dioxide it needed. It's having the exchange of oxygen and carbon dioxide—and compact soil can't get the exchange of gases. When the exchange is all balanced, everything just flourishes."

He explained that his wife, Karen, a licensed nurse nutritionist, became so concerned about the dead soil caused by years of chemical use on the family farm that they decided to trade industrial farming practices for organic and biodynamic methods of restoring life to the family's rice fields. This encouraged the living soil even more. Kurt took the change one step further—he even processes his rice differently. "I just take the hull off the rice. I leave the grain with the bran and the germ—all the nutrition in it."

I saw that mixed in with the brown jasmine rice were tiny disc-shaped red grains. When I asked Kurt about them, he explained that those red discs are the bane of most rice growers who traditionally use chemicals in their rice fields to kill it. "It's just a native grass, a rice that's crossed," he continued. "Crossed" rice indicates that two species have genetically combined, resulting in a new variety—in this case, the commercial rice mixed with a wild rice. The federal government actually refers to it as a noxious weed, but Kurt refers to the red grains as "a blessing from God."

"It grows on its own, so it's very, very hard to manage. It has a shorter maturity date and a shattering problem. When it grows, it falls off on the ground. It's very hard to manage it, but sometimes things just work out right. I guess the good Lord makes things work for some reason. I did some insect control by removing the water, but when I did that, it allowed the red rice to come up. But the timing! It came up at the right time, so I had it in my rice and the customers have just loved it! In fact, I get customers who want me to take the white rice out and just send the red rice to them, but I can't do that!" He laughed.

How does the rice farmer prefer to eat his rice? Kurt likes to add a minced garlic clove to the rice and water before cooking. He stirs a big pat of Smith's Creamery butter into the cooked rice with a generous sprinkling of aged grated cheese for a satisfying, meatless meal. Risotto is usually made with Italian Arborio rice, but with a slight modification in technique, this unique brown rice makes a fantastic variation.

Cajun Grain is also Kurt's favorite way to start the day. "I eat it for breakfast. I run it through the coffee grinder, and then I mix half oatmeal and half rice together with water to cook it. I add whatever I have in the house—blueberries, sunflower seeds, pecans, or pumpkin seeds. By the time you've had your cup of coffee, it's ready, and it's so good with a little honey on top that I can't wait to get up in the morning! I really like to add the goat yogurt on top. I used to always eat it hot, but now I eat a little bit hot then put it in the refrigerator and come back and eat it cold," he continued enthusiastically.

Besides growing rice, Kurt and Karen have raised three children on the farm alongside grass-fed cattle, free-range pigs, and a vegetable plot. The vitality of their life on the farm is evident in Kurt's excitement when describing the delicious life they lead and nurture in their communities.

Kurt Unkel's Brown Jasmine Rice and Oatmeal Cereal

Here's Kurt's recipe for his favorite way to start the day on the farm.

Yields 2 servings

6 tbsp. brown jasmine rice
¼ tsp. salt
2 cups water

½ cup quick-cook (not instant) oatmeal
Butter, honey, milk, flax seed, sunflower seeds, or pumpkin seeds, for garnish, if desired

In a clean coffee grinder or food processor, grind brown jasmine rice until coarsely chopped.

Bring salt and water to a boil in a 2½-quart saucepan.

Stir in rice and oatmeal. Reduce heat to low and cover. Simmer together, stirring periodically, for 10 minutes or until thickened. Garnish how you like and serve immediately.

Louisiana Brown Jasmine Rice and Artichoke Risotto

Here's one of my favorite ways to cook Kurt's Cajun Grain. It's a great side dish for grilled or roasted meats or makes for a satisfying meatless meal all on its own!

Yields 4 servings

4 tbsp. butter, divided
1 cup brown jasmine rice
2½ cups chicken stock, divided
½ cup chopped onion
1 clove garlic, minced

½ cup dry white wine
1 14-oz. can quartered artichoke hearts
¼ cup grated parmesan or Romano cheese
Salt and black pepper to taste

Melt 2 tbsp. of the butter in a 2½-quart saucepan. Add rice and stir over medium heat for 2 to 3 minutes until rice is well coated with butter and begins to smell nutty. Add 2 cups chicken stock; bring to a boil. Cover pot; reduce heat to low; and cook undisturbed for 25 minutes. Remove from heat and reserve.

In a 3½-quart saucepan, melt the remaining 2 tbsp. butter. Add the onion and garlic; cook over medium heat until the onion is translucent, about 4 minutes.

In a separate bowl, combine the white wine with the remaining ½ cup chicken stock. Pour half of the combined liquids over the sautéed onions and bring to a simmer. Stir in the artichoke hearts and the cooked rice and cook, stirring continuously, adding more of the wine mixture as needed. When all the liquid is absorbed, stir in the grated cheese and season to taste with salt and pepper. Serve at once.

Big Boys Do Cry

The first time I laid eyes on Brett Anderson he had been writing for the *New Orleans Times-Picayune* for less than a year, and, like most New Orleanians, I was carefully reading every word he wrote to see if this kid—an outsider from Minnesota—could possibly "get" us.

He'd succeeded Sumi Hahn as the newspaper's restaurant critic, and the two are linked in my mind for a very special reason. Sumi once was also an outsider, but I'd enjoyed her fresh take on our food scene, and in 1999, she introduced me to the international Slow Food movement in a *Times-Picayune* article focusing on Slow Food's Ark of Taste concept. In the piece, Sumi had queried, "What are New Orleans' endangered foods?"

This caught my attention, as I'd already been involved for years in helping to protect and preserve our authentic foods through my Louisiana-centric cooking classes. In Sumi's article, I discovered that there was an international organization out there, just waiting to help me.

I picked up the phone and called Slow Food's main offices in Italy, asking, "How do you start a local Slow Food chapter?" Then, I called Sumi to thank her for writing the piece. She responded by thanking me, saying that when she wrote, she always hoped there was a reader out there who would be inspired by her words.

All of New Orleans grasped the Ark concept and the local chapter quickly began nominating and welcoming endangered foods that we all agreed New Orleans could not bear to lose—and that were, in fact, endangered—onto our virtual Noah's ark.

Creole cream cheese was the first food to galvanize the chapter, and it remains one of the US Slow Food Ark's greatest success stories. In 1999, Dorignac's Food Center was the sole remaining producer of Creole cream cheese, a recipe that they made themselves. The local dairies that once had produced the soft, single-curd cheese gradually had been bought out by large, out-of-state operations, whose management did not understand the importance of the cheese that New Orleanians had eaten for breakfast and enjoyed frozen for dessert since the earliest days of the city.

Largely because of the focus that our Slow Food chapter had placed on Creole cream cheese, the Mauthe family, who operates a small family dairy farm on the north shore of Lake Pontchartrain, decided to begin making the cheese. They first sold their Creole cream cheese at the then relatively new Crescent City Farmers Market on Saturday, August 2, 2001.

In my mind, this was going to be the litmus test for the *Times-Picayune*'s new food writer. In advance of the Mauthes' first day at the farmers market, I called Brett and told him I had a really big food story for him and tried to explain what Creole cream cheese was and what it meant to the city. I invited him to my home in July 2001 for a tasting and to meet the dairy farmer who was about to rescue our beloved local food. That was how Brett Anderson found himself at my kitchen table.

From the very first look, I was fascinated by the tall, gangly young man, whose quick wit and intelligence were immediately evident through the dark, horn-rimmed glasses he wore. He reminded me of Clark Kent and, in fact, he was about to turn into my Superman.

Once Brett heard Kenny Mauthe's story and tasted his Creole cream cheese, he agreed to write a piece about the new marketing plan that the Mauthes hoped would save the family farm. Brett's article ran in the Thursday food section of the *Times-Picayune* on July 31, 2001.

The motivation to go into production of Creole cream cheese at the Mauthe's dairy farm came from a desperate need to hang on to the fourth generation's tradition of dairy farming. Because of the effects of the commodity market, the small dairy farmer today has an extremely difficult time making a profit. Commodity prices bear little relation to the farm's actual production costs. That is why the Louisiana dairy farm in general has become endangered.

Brett's piece turned into a two-page spread, complete with color photos of those beautiful Jersey cows that produced the milk and cream for the cream cheese. The piece appeared in the Thursday food section of the *Times-Picayune,* announcing that the Mauthes would be at the Saturday Crescent City Farmers Market with real Creole cream cheese to sell.

That morning, eager buyers lined up around the block awaiting the 8 a.m. opening bell. The Mauthes arrived with five hundred cartons of Creole cream cheese and were completely sold out by 10 a.m., beginning a craze that led many other small dairies—and even Chef John Folse—to begin manufacturing this early passenger of Slow Food USA's Ark of Taste.

I was already smitten with Brett after he helped save Creole cream cheese, but I think I fell in love with my restaurant-critic Superman when he wrote a piece entitled "Dinner with Moth," which appeared in the September 25, 2001, issue of the *Times-Picayune*. The entire country was still reeling from the horror of what had happened two weeks prior on 9/11.

In the article, Brett reminisced about his first dining experience at Galatoire's, a New Orleans institution whose archaic charms first seduced Brett less than three weeks into his new life here. It was an experience he intended to share with his high school buddy Gordy "Moth" Aamoth when Moth came to New Orleans later in the fall. Their fun was going to include an LSU football game and a leisurely Friday Galatoire's lunch.

But on September 11, 2001, as Brett watched the Twin

Towers of the World Trade Center crumble on television, his New York banker friend was on the 104th floor of Tower 2. Brett knew that he would miss that Friday lunch at Galatoire's. Brett reported that, "angry at the monsters who did this terrible thing," he dealt with the crushing grief by returning to lunch at Galatoire's, heartbroken that he and Moth would never share a plate of the soufflé potatoes they had discussed ordering. He did not allow the terrorists to keep him from dinner with his friend; instead of sitting across from one another, Brett recalled the memories that he and Moth shared together. This was the first time that a *Times-Picayune* food article made me cry.

During the ensuing decade that Brett wrote for the *Times-Picayune,* our friendship grew. Brett protected his anonymity as a restaurant critic by using pseudonyms when he made reservations and by paying with credit cards in other names, but anyone who'd ever heard his wacky, distinctive laugh knew who he was.

When it was announced on May 24, 2012, that the 175-year-old New Orleans daily newspaper intended to reduce publication to three days a week and cut much of the staff, my friend Brett was one of the first writers from whom I wanted to hear. I knew that he'd received a prestigious fellowship from the Nieman Foundation for Journalism and intended to spend a year at Harvard University that fall. I called Brett and asked if he'd be willing to talk with me on *Louisiana Eats!* about the changes at the newspaper. After spurting a string of expletives to describe how he felt personally about the situation, he said, "Hell, yes!"

That's how I found myself sitting across from Brett in the studio. It was a hot summer day and Brett was dressed in his usual attire, a pair of baggy jeans and a tee-shirt. I began by asking him how he'd come to be a food writer in the first place. "I got my first job at a weekly newspaper in Minneapolis, when I was still in college, where I was a rock music writer, which, at that point in my life, was my life's ambition," he answered. His editor in Minneapolis brought Brett along with him to another paper in Washington, DC, and suggested that he write about food as well. Brett began to write a column called *Young and Hungry.*

He described his credentials at that time as "a critical voice that would serve food and restaurants well, and a natural curiosity, but most of all, a voracious appetite. I was pretty young at the time and known to be able to put it away.

"I did that job for five years and as it went along, the food part of it gradually became more of my professional identity than I would have guessed it would have been," he continued. "My ambition was not to end up writing about food full-time; it was to be a magazine writer or a general news assignment reporter. But as time went on, that particular beat felt pretty bottomless in terms of the stories that it provided. And having come to it from the perspective of someone who was very much a neophyte, coming from the Midwest and not a very food-crazed background, really served me well in some ways, because I had so much to learn. I still feel like I've hardly even scratched the surface. As a journalist and just a naturally curious person, that's a really exciting position to be in."

He described getting the job at the *Times-Picayune* as "still sort of a mystery to me." Brett ruminated that "at that time, the newspaper industry itself was much larger with a lot more jobs out there for food writers. Attracting someone with a lot of experience would have been harder. I can understand how they were looking for someone who was younger and they thought might stick around."

Here in New Orleans, Brett thrived. Aside from his work for the *Times-Picayune,* his writing appeared in *Gourmet,* the *Washington Post, Food and Wine,* and *Salon.* Along the way, he won ten awards from the Association of Food Journalists and a James Beard Foundation Journalism Award.

The way Brett saw it, "The best thing about my job is not that I get to eat out all the time for free; it's that I get to write about a topic that this city is so closely identified with—that people are so fascinated with. Food is really something that defines New Orleans, and there's an audience that really loves food and appears to really love reading about food. You get to write for an audience that believes there's something at stake."

I asked Brett why he thought New Orleans food always seemed to stay the same and why everyone here felt they had a stake in it, and he admitted that he had theories. He told me that when he had to give a talk once at a Southern Foodways Alliance Symposium in Oxford, Mississippi, about what New Orleans music had taught him about New Orleans food, he'd realized that being such a serious and avid music lover had helped him, as an outsider, learn New Orleans' unique culture more quickly and had helped him to understand the food, too.

"There's a culture in both food and music where there's a respect for the canon," he said. "When you learn the standards, there's an art to that and you can express your own artistic voice and your own personality by interpreting work that has been handed down over generations in your own way. I really see New Orleans food—especially the classic recipes you see everywhere—through that lens. It took me a long time to get that but I think there's a strong tradition here of upholding tradition and I think it's a beautiful thing.

"I've been here for eleven years now and, particularly in the last five, we've seen in New Orleans restaurants a lot of creativity that still pays a certain respect to the tradition that I find pretty exciting. An obvious example is what Donald Link and Stephen Stryjewski have been up to at Cochon, where they have taken Cajun cuisine and they've sort of cleaned it up without fancying it up—that makes you realize we haven't even scratched the surface of this food. They bring modern techniques to the table there but not in a way that's terribly corrupting. How you can create a modern restaurant that satisfies what everything that a serious diner expects from a modern American restaurant while working completely within a tradition," he said.

Then, I asked about his favorite New Orleans food memory. At first, he thought I was just asking where he'd had the finest meal and glibly answered that there were too many to choose from. So I clarified that it was the food memories he'd acquired here that he'd be taking with him to Harvard that I wanted to know about.

There was a long pause, and when Brett began speaking again, it was clear he was fighting back tears. He said, "Acquiring an accumulation of taste memories that makes me feel like, when I taste something, it tastes like a place, is really valuable to me—a collection of memories that I understand as something that is a single entity in a sense. If I was to leave—to move away from New Orleans and come back for a weekend—I've got a list of restaurants that I'd want to go to and they tend to be the old-fashioned ones that you can't find anything like them in other places."

He paused again, and I watched as the food memories washed over him and he wiped his eyes with the hem of his tee-shirt before continuing, "Galatoire's, Brigtsen's, Clancy's, the Upperline." His voice trailed off and he took a deep sigh then continued, "Or the roast beef poor boys at R & O's. I've become so aware that the experiences that those restaurants give are so singular to New Orleans itself. There's a lot of places in New Orleans that do that. Those are the places I'd really want to continue to create memories at."

Then, we moved on to the situation at the *Times-Picayune*. He told me that he was in New York on a week's vacation when word of the changes had leaked out. The news of Brett's status at the paper had been particularly confusing; it was initially reported that Brett would be handed a pink slip, but shortly thereafter, the official word from Jim Amoss, the paper's publisher, was that Brett might be coming back to his job at the *Times-Picayune* after his year at Harvard.

I asked how there could have been a misunderstanding about whether he'd been fired or not. "I don't want to belabor that point, mainly because I wasn't the only person laid off that day, so I don't think that my being laid off should be thought of as being any more disappointing or tragic than anyone else's. And, I was offered an opportunity to come back, so I don't feel right picking at that wound," he said.

"The people who work there and have been charged with making these changes have been given an overwhelming amount of responsibilities, so in the process there will be mistakes made and miscommunications. One explanation I was given was that if they had not severed me they would have had to fire someone else, and you know, inasmuch as that is the case, I think it was the right thing to do."

The paper's cuts were another emotional issue for both the city and Brett. He paused, and wiped his eyes again.

Composing himself, he continued, "It's obvious that the daily-newspaper model just doesn't exist anymore as it once did. We can all agree that something had to be done to preserve daily journalism in major markets, but whether it was the right thing—history will have to be the judge of that."

Trying to lighten things up, I asked what he was looking forward to about attending Harvard. Brett said he wanted to study and research the people and forces that gave rise to modern celebrity chef culture. He went on, "We're living in a very transformative time when it comes to food in America, and the rise of food into mainstream American culture has been quite stunning. My interest in that really stems from the fact that New Orleans has played a crucial role in that cultural development, most obviously with Paul Prudhomme and Emeril Lagasse, but I want to research all the players in that. And after living through Katrina and the BP oil spill, maybe I'll study the mental health of disasters on communities." Then, laughing that distinctive laugh, he said, "And I also want someone to explain Faulkner to me."

Then I asked what Brett's perfect world might look like after the Neiman fellowship, and he said, "In my perfect world, I get to live in New Orleans, be a working journalist and writer in New Orleans writing about New Orleans."

For those of us who love New Orleans and New Orleans food and have come to love the gawky, lanky guy with the crazy laugh who is Brett Anderson, that hope is part of our perfect world, too.

Creole Cream Cheese

Here's the recipe for New Orleans' beloved Creole cream cheese, whose cause Brett helped champion with his pen.

Yields approximately 8 pints

1 gal. skim milk
1 cup buttermilk
Pinch salt

6-8 drops liquid vegetable rennet (can be purchased in health food stores)

In a large stainless steel or glass bowl, combine all ingredients. Cover lightly with plastic wrap and leave out on kitchen counter at room temperature for 18 to 24 hours. You will then find one large cheese curd floating in whey.

Take 8 pint-sized cheese molds (or make your own) and a slotted spoon and spoon large pieces of the cheese into the molds. Put molds on a rack in a roasting pan and again cover lightly with plastic wrap; refrigerate. Allow cheese to drain for 6 to 8 hours before turning them out of molds. To serve, pour a bit of cream or half-and-half on top of the cheese and sprinkle with sugar, or eat savory-style—sprinkled with kosher salt and freshly ground black pepper. The cheese can be stored in a tightly covered container for up to 2 weeks.

Crabmeat Ravigote

Here's my version of a classic Galatoire's dish that Brett had planned to enjoy at his meal with his friend Moth.

Yields 4-6 servings as a first course

Juice of 1 lemon
1 egg
1 cup oil
1 lb. lump crabmeat
6 oz. capers, drained and chopped

3 tbsp. chopped parsley
6-8 green onions, thinly sliced
Salt, pepper, and hot sauce to taste
1 head iceberg lettuce, finely sliced

Combine lemon juice and egg in a food processor. With the machine running, slowly drizzle in oil until well combined and resembles mayonnaise.

In a large bowl, combine egg mixture, crab, capers, parsley, and green onions. Season to taste with salt, black pepper, and hot sauce. Chill thoroughly and serve on a bed of lettuce.

Lance Hill to the Rescue

Dr. Lance Hill's day job is serving as the executive director of the Southern Institute for Education and Research at Tulane University. It's a formidable title, and he does important work there, having been especially instrumental in breaking down local race barriers through efforts such as sensitivity training with the New Orleans police force. But his work as an educator was not what brought us together.

Lance also is a crop conservationist, a food folklorist, and the founder of the Adopt-a-Mirliton Project. His mission? Saving Louisiana's heirloom mirliton.

Depending on where you live, you may call the mirliton by any of three to four hundred different names. In Latin, it is *Sechium edule*. There is even a Chinese character for the pear shaped, sometimes prickly, sometimes smooth, ovoid edible that's identified as both a vegetable and fruit, depending on culture and preparation. In the United States, where it appears in the produce section of many supermarkets, it is best known by its Spanish name,

chayote. Despite its profusion of names and the part it plays in food cultures across the globe, many people have no idea whatsoever about what this food is.

Lance's efforts to save the Louisiana heirloom mirliton began after Hurricane Katrina in 2005, when it became clear that the plant was endangered. Lance's mission quickly caught the attention of Richard McCarthy and the Crescent City Farmers Market.

In 2008, the market became an agricultural incubator of sorts when they agreed to host the Adopt-a-Mirliton Project on marketumbrella.org, which helped grow the Crescent City Farmers Market, and donate space for events to distribute the rare plants. Today, all of this is maintained by Lance at its own Web site.

"What happened in New Orleans: all the mirlitons were destroyed by Katrina, because mirlitons cannot survive more than 24 to 48 hours underwater, so the flood waters wiped out a tremendous number of backyard mirlitons," he explained. "Wind damage can actually traumatize a plant so that it won't flower. Then a hard freeze can kill it."

Mirlitons have to be protected in a hard freeze, which, luckily, is rare in New Orleans. The hard freeze in 1995 wiped out a lot of the local varieties before the hurricane of 2005. "When there's a hard freeze—unless they are protected by two or three feet of mulch and sometimes carpet—they'll die. So, it is quite possible that we could lose a traditional variety if we're not careful to cultivate it and spread it out around the region so it's not susceptible to extinction."

After observing how many Louisiana heirloom mirliton vines the hurricane and its resulting floodwaters destroyed, Lance set out to find growers in Louisiana who still had mirliton vines and who might donate or sell seed mirlitons to other growers in order to prevent total extinction.

Lance credits the *New Orleans Times-Picayune* food editor, Judy Walker, for really jumpstarting his Adopt-A-Mirliton program. "Most of the heirlooms we found happened through a reverse process when the *Times-Picayune* did a story about our project. The story was republished in the agricultural extension newsletter and I had people call me who were growing different varieties. The calls came—especially from Acadiana. So, I began to travel through South Lafourche, what is called 'the saltwater parish,' up through Acadiana. I found nine different mirlitons, including a pure white one, which is very beautiful and is grown in Opelousas. In Cajun country, the mirliton is called a 'mallytone' and they even spell it that way!

"We have identified nine varieties that have been grown long enough—100 to 150 years—and can be considered an heirloom," Lance said. "To identify traditionally grown mirlitons, we do the history. We interview people whose families have planted them for 70 to 80 years. We do site visits to ensure that they're not affected by disease and not using fungicides. And we see how well they produce. Then it's a judgment call to say, 'This is what we will call an heirloom traditional Louisiana mirliton.' We have also found we have a much better success rate growing those."

As soon as I'd grasped the distinctive qualities of the Louisiana heirloom mirliton and understood its endangered status, I nominated it to the Slow Food USA Ark of Taste. The committee voted to board it, pending the necessary tasting notes. The problem was finding one of the rare heirloom mirlitons to taste.

I brought a Vermont friend and Slow Food Ark of Taste colleague, Robin Schempp, with me to Lance's office on the Tulane campus to hear his mirliton stories and to beg for one of the precious seed mirlitons to officially evaluate its taste and compile the necessary notes for the committee's review.

The imposing, bearded figure that is Lance Hill was situated behind his huge wooden desk. He regaled us with amazing mirliton facts as we talked (and talked, and talked) that long fall afternoon. Robin and I took reams of notes and, later, carefully tasted a rare Mr. Rock mirliton with almost religious fervor. After reviewing our tasting notes, the Ark of Taste committee gave the Louisiana heirloom mirliton its final nod of approval and it is now officially internationally recognized as a valuable part of our cultural food heritage.

Although we in the South consider it part of our culture—and rightly so—in our *Louisiana Eats!* interview, Lance explained that the mirliton is not native to the United States. "It originated 60 million years ago in Asia, then it spread as the continent spread. They float in typhoons and hurricanes, so mirlitons that are two million years old are found in Hawaii.

"They were first cultivated in Mesoamerica and Central America," Lance continued. "The one that came to be known as the chayote is probably the one that's the most hybridized. It came up from Central America to New Orleans through an interesting route, which we don't know exactly.

"The only other place it's called 'mirliton' is in Haiti, in the place once called Santo Domingo, and sometimes in France, where the word 'mirliton' can also mean a hat, a candy, or a soldier. There's even a town in France called Mirliton."

Through his research, Lance has tracked its cultivation in Louisiana as far back 1840. It's always referred to as a 'mirliton' in Louisiana archives. Lance theorizes that "in 1804, there was a revolution on the island of Haiti and about five thousand Creoles of color—the *gens de couleur libres*—had to flee the island. They came to New Orleans and settled in what now is called Treme. They brought with them the traditional cuisine of the mirliton.

"The eight or nine varieties that have been here one to two hundred years, like humans, develop a resistance to certain specific diseases and are more tolerant to coastal climates. The ones we have here came from the Caribbean and are a little more tolerant to rain, a little more tolerant to sun and anthracnose, a common fungus," he continued.

The reason that Lance has successfully been able to reseed the area is because "growers donate them to us. I have bought some with my own personal funds, but a lot of people will just donate. When we allow someone to adopt an heirloom plant that we've propagated, we expect them to donate half of their crop back for seed," he explained.

While Hurricane Katrina did major damage to local crops, the Louisiana heirloom mirliton had been in trouble for a long time. Lance also credits New Orleans' lack of traditional varieties to bad advice. Fifteen or twenty years ago, when hybridized South American mirlitons began to be sold commonly in groceries, local horticulturists advised people who wanted to grow a mirliton to buy one at the supermarket and plant it. But people who cultivated grocery store mirlitons discovered that it took a lot of pesticides and fungicides to successfully grow those here. And, as Lance noted, "The difference between the four-thousand-foot altitude of Costa Rica and here, where we're twelve feet below sea level, makes quite a different environment."

Lance and I agree that another reason the mirliton began to fade as a popular New Orleans plant was the demise of the once-popular page fence, often referred to here as a "hurricane fence." The metal fence provided a perfect trellis and also made for a great visual neighborhood improvement as the large, bright green leaves thickly covered the unattractive aluminum fences.

Lance bemoaned the lack of taste in non-native mirlitons. "The imported cultigens from Costa Rica, Mexico, and Argentina are different in flavor and texture. The growers have hybridized them for what they call 'insipid flavor.' Those mirlitons are uniform in shape and color. They're not troughed and they don't have prickles and they have no flavor," he said.

"For instance, with the Mr. Rock variety, you'll discover that some of them have tremendous flavor. The difference is in the morphology of the fruit."

It's hard to describe the flavor, but Lance uses the term 'crystalline,' often used to define wines. "It's not sweet, not sour—it's sort of indescribable. The cucumber is in the same family (the cucurbit family) so, in ways, they are similar. They tend to have this kind of crisp, light flavor, which tends to compliment certain kinds of flavors complemented by limes or in heavier sauces. It's a question of how intense the flavor is, and, also, the texture can be different depending on the mirliton," he said.

Once he began to talk about taste, he expansively noted that, "The international ways that people consume mirliton is what is really fun." He discovered that by using "Google Translate," he could take all the names for the mirliton that he'd found on Wikipedia and translate them from the 80 different languages notated.

For instance, he said, "I put in the word *sayote,* the Phillipino word, did a search, and found recipes for how mirlitons are used in the Philippines, where it is an essential part of the cuisine. They use them to make candy, and that's where I found a recipe for mirliton French fries. They are cut up like fries, then parboiled, then fried in a kind of tempura batter."

Lance pointed out the elevated status the simple mirliton has had for generations on Reunion, an island northeast of mainland Africa in the Seychelles. In the seventeenth century, the slaves retreated into the mountainous region of the island, bringing the mirlitons with them. Today, they grow "like Kudzu" on hillsides. He continued the story. "At some point in the eighteenth century, the poor white farmers were also driven into those same mountains by the plantation owners. There, they intermarried with the runaway slaves, creating an authentic Creole culture, complete with its own distinctive patois.

"The mirliton actually is worshiped on that island," he said. "In those parts of the world, they eat the leaves and the tendrils in salads and stir-fries," he said. The slaves eventually figured out how to even weave a type of fabric with the mirliton, and they even used it to make hats." Little wonder it became a sacred plant.

In addition, Lance pointed out, "You can actually make mirliton wine. We have found a local vintner who is willing to make us forty gallons—but that's a lot of mirliton juice!"

His personal relationship with the mirliton dates back almost thirty years to his early days in New Orleans, when he came here from Kansas. "When we first lived here, we lived in Algiers," he mused. "I believe pecans make neighbors hate neighbors, but mirlitons make neighbors love neighbors. I had a pecan tree in Algiers and people steal your pecans. Kids throw things at pecan trees to get at the nuts. But I had a neighbor who had a single mirliton vine that would produce over 150 mirlitons. Abundance makes you generous. Neighbors who don't even talk to neighbors will show up at the front door with sack of fifty mirlitons and say, 'Do you want them?'"

Along with the abundance of mirlitons, the Algiers neighbor also gave him his first mirliton recipe. "It was for mirliton pie. It's sweet like a banana bread," he reported.

With a story like that, maybe if everyone grew mirlitons, it would result in world peace!

Salade de Xuxu

Although it's rare in New Orleans, in other parts of the world the mirliton is frequently eaten raw in salads. You will be pleasantly surprised at the refreshing, delicious taste of this Brazilian mirliton and orange salad—a perfect seasonal combination for fall and winter.

Yields 4 servings

2 raw mirlitons
3 oranges
1 tbsp. extra virgin olive oil
Juice of 2 limes
Salt and pepper to taste
1 bunch green onions, sliced
Fresh coriander, parsley, or mint, finely chopped, for
   garnish

Peel and seed the mirlitons. Rub them under cold running water to eliminate their natural stickiness. Shred the mirliton with a grater into a large bowl.

Peel and supreme the oranges, reserving any juice that leaks. Add to grated mirlitons.

Make a dressing by combining the olive oil, lime juice, and reserved orange juice, and season with salt and pepper. Toss the dressing with the orange sections, the shredded mirliton, and the green onions. Chill for at least 30 minutes. Before serving, toss salad again. Sprinkle with fresh coriander, parley, or mint, and serve.

Mirliton Fries

Lance has morphed this basic recipe into creative "flights of fritters" and such—but here is his original for the fries.

Yields about 2 servings

1 large mirliton
1 cup finely ground rice flour
1 cup all-purpose flour
1 tsp. salt
Scant tsp. ground turmeric

⅛ tsp. ground mustard
¼ tsp. paprika
Pinch of cayenne pepper
Ice water, as needed
Oil for frying

Peel and slice the mirliton into fry-sized pieces. Parboil the fries in boiling water for 10 minutes or until tender on the outside and firm inside.

In a large bowl, combine the rice flour, all-purpose flour, salt, turmeric, mustard, paprika, and cayenne. Add just enough ice water to make a smooth batter. Drop the mirliton slices into the mixture and make sure that all are coated. Refrigerate for 15 to 20 minutes or until just ready to cook and serve.

Heat the oil for frying. Fry the mirliton for a few minutes, until it begins to get a nice golden color. Drain on paper towels and serve immediately.

Note: Instead of the flours and turmeric, you can substitute with commercial tempura mix.

Seafood-Stuffed Mirlitons

The favorite way to prepare mirlitons in Louisiana is stuffed with any combination of seasonings and gulf seafood. The subtle flavor of the mirliton provides a perfect showcase for those luxurious ingredients. My seafood-stuffed mirlitons are an annual favorite on our family's holiday table. I also like to freeze stuffed mirlitons as a quick, re-heatable main course for dinner.

Yields 8 servings

4 mirlitons
½ cup butter, plus additional for topping
1 yellow onion, finely chopped
½ lb. shrimp, peeled, chopped
2 tbsp. diced ham

½ lb. crab claw meat
6-8 green onions, thinly sliced
¼ cup seasoned breadcrumbs, plus additional for topping
Salt and black pepper to taste

Cut each mirliton in half lengthwise and boil in salted water until just tender. Remove and discard the seed. Scoop out the mirliton with a spoon, carefully preserving the shell and reserving the meat.

Preheat oven to 350 degrees. Melt the butter in a skillet. Add the yellow onion and sauté until translucent. Add the mirliton meat. Stir in shrimp and cook until just pink, about 2 minutes. Remove from heat and add ham, crabmeat, green onions, and breadcrumbs. Season with salt and pepper to taste.

Fill mirliton halves with stuffing. Sprinkle with additional breadcrumbs and top with pats of additional butter. Bake for 20 to 25 minutes, or until heated through.

Photograph courtesy David Gallent

Keeping Kosher: Creole and Cajun Style

Keeping kosher in south Louisiana can be a daunting task, considering the overwhelming presence of pork and shellfish—both forbidden in kosher kitchens but essential in Creole and Cajun cuisine.

Mildred Covert grew up in a Creole kosher household and has continued to keep kosher her entire life. The innovative adaptations of local flavors that began with her Polish immigrant grandmother eventually inspired Mildred to co-author, with her friend Sylvia Gerson, many books, including *Kosher Creole Cooking* and *Kosher Cajun Cooking*. These seminal works are still beloved by kosher cooks everywhere.

Having the opportunity to interview Mildred on *Louisiana Eats!* was another dream come true for me. We have known each other since our days together at Lee Barnes Cooking School, where Mildred worked her kosher Creole and Cajun magic in classes that always filled up quickly. Occasionally, I was lucky enough to be her assistant.

Even today, Mildred marvels at the courage of her grandmother, Hinde Ester Kleinfeldt, who traveled alone with her five small children from a little town in Poland to America. Mildred describes her family background as typical of those days, with her grandfather coming over to America first and working until he earned enough money to send for his wife and children. Mildred's grandfather had worked for a year as a shoemaker until he was able to send for his family.

Keeping kosher in America was a whole new game for Mildred's grandmother. She had to adapt to new surroundings armed with a laundry list of prohibited foods to keep out of her kitchen. However, the challenges of balancing an old religion with a new culture and language were many—and they began the moment the family stepped foot on American ground.

Mildred's grandmother entered the country through Ellis Island, where she saw her first banana. Mildred told me, "She saw a man selling bananas on the dock. Knowing she had five children to feed, she watched the man peeling the banana. It looked like something that could be kosher, as nothing had touched a pot or a pan, so she decided to buy some bananas to see if the children would eat them. Sure enough, they liked the bananas, so she went back to the man on the dock and gave him another, larger, coin, which was a nickel, thinking she would get more bananas.

"Her first purchase had been made with a dime. Having no previous experience with American money, she thought she'd been cheated and began to protest loudly," Mildred chuckled, recalling the ruckus she must have made. "Someone there on the dock explained to her the difference between a dime and a nickel. My grandmother told me that was how she learned about the American dollar."

Once in New Orleans, Mildred's grandmother's culinary adventures continued. At the time, she believed, as did many Old World Europeans, that the tomato was poisonous. "She had never fooled with tomatoes. Another thing that amazes you when you speak about adapting to surroundings: she quickly learned to use the tomato. In fact, for years I don't think I ever remember a roast coming out of the oven without a tomato sauce on it!" Mildred said with a slight groan of complaint.

"As things got more comfortable for us, we had a young African American woman named Pearl who came to work for us," Mildred continued. "She couldn't have been more than seventeen or eighteen years old. She came from Hazelhurst, Mississippi, and remained with us for forty-five years," Mildred remembered fondly.

Her grandmother would supervise Pearl, "so that in our household, without realizing it, this culinary change of the real South soul food and the Creole taste and the seasonings were all beginning to be infused in the food we were eating, yet it was still kosher."

"When it came to the red beans and rice, which to this day I still eat on Monday—remember, I was born here—of course, a ham hock or anything like that were completely forbidden. So Grandmother showed Pearl how to take a piece of corned beef brisket and use that for seasoning, or a kosher smoked sausage, and so, to this day, that's what we use to season. But the real seasonings—the parsley, the thyme, the celery, bell pepper, and onion—all of this is kosher. It's just knowing what to blend with what and you still have that flavor," Mildred said.

Reflecting on some of the city's great dishes, such as Chicken Clemenceau, Mildred told me, "I have often said, 'What's the difference if I use a kosher chicken?' I have the original Galatoire's recipe and I still use it today for special occasions."

The culinary adventures were not without their hiccups. When Mildred and Sylvia Gerson, her co-author and friend, did their very first cooking demonstration to promote the first book, they "decided to get really fancy and make what we called a 'Mock Oyster Rockefeller,'" Mildred remembered.

"Everything in the Rockefeller sauce is kosher, but of course there is no oyster in the kosher kitchen. So we took pieces of gefilte fish and sliced it to the size of an oyster. We did it completely with the rock salt, the shells, everything. The problem was that the oven we had to use was the store's convection oven, which neither of us had ever used before."

She thought everything was fine until the shoppers came to taste. Mildred noticed as they took bites of the Rockefeller, they put napkins to their mouths, spitting it out and throwing it in the trashcan. When Mildred tasted it to see what was wrong, she discovered, "It was nothing but brine!" The blowing heat of the convection oven had actually blown the rock salt on top of the Rockefeller, making it too salty to eat.

When it comes to holiday feasting, Mildred's cooking really shines. She thinks that Hanukkah is the best Jewish holiday to celebrate in New Orleans, culinarily speaking. "We are so known for our fried foods here: beignets, fried seafood. Hanukkah is really all about oil. We do our famous potato latke, but there are so many other foods we can make in New Orleans to celebrate Hanukkah.

"I have made carrot fritters, apple fritters, banana fritters, corn fritters—all these great Southern things that you drop into that hot oil. It's the oil that's symbolic of Hanukkah—not the potato! After all, potatoes didn't even reach Europe until the 1500s, when they were brought over from South America, so that originally, biblically, the first latke was the pancake that was made back in 165 BC. The women only had flour and water to work with, to cook something for the men who were in battle," Mildred reported.

New Orleans' Passover foods are yet another of Mildred's passions—luckily, because the dietary laws are even more strict. "It's hectic, because to keep Passover the home has to be cleansed of all foods that are forbidden to be eaten during the eight-day festival. We have our own separate dishes and pots and pans, etcetera, in order to cook and prepare for the Passover seder. I think it's the most celebrated of all Jewish holidays regardless of how observant you might be. Even though I am born here in New Orleans and really addicted to Creole and Cajun food, when it comes to Passover, it is such a solemn holiday and restricted in so many culinary ways that it does become difficult to fuse in some Creole or Cajun cooking. But one way or another, I have always found a way

to sneak a little into the Passover kitchen," Mildred said.

"For instance, you can use tomatoes in Passover, and I've used matzo meal instead of cornmeal to make fried green tomatoes and topping it with gefilte fish sauced with a remoulade. Usually gefilte fish is made with pike, but down South, my grandmother always made her gefilte fish with fresh trout and redfish."

Mildred described how she buys pre-made gefilte fish balls, rolls them in matzo crumbs, drops them into hot oil, and when they are browned, she serves them as hors d'oeuvres, a "Passover Crab Ball."

Many a Passover guest has been surprised to hear that Mildred was serving Passover Pain Perdu for dessert. Any leavened bread is expressly forbidden during Passover, but a commercially available Passover pound cake provided the perfect "pain" for the "perdu." "I slice it an inch thick, use the same eggs and milk, and fry it in a little butter with powdered sugar sprinkled on top and have it for dessert!" Mildred laughed.

Another of Mildred's Passover specialties is a matzo Napoleon layered with chocolate pudding, matzos, and fresh strawberries. "It softens a little when it sits and you just cut it up, and there you have it!" she said.

Washington, DC,-based author Joan Nathan has pursued the DNA of Jewish cookery in many books. She has traveled the world in this relentless pursuit, tracing the roots of her heritage's cuisine across Europe, Africa, and Asia. From the north to the South Pole, Joan has not left a stone unturned in her meticulous research.

Joan authored *Jewish Cooking in America,* which won both the James Beard Award and the IACP/Julia Child Cookbook of the Year Award in 1994. When Joan came to New Orleans on tour with her latest book, *Quiches, Kugels, and Couscous,* I was lucky enough to snag her for a studio interview.

Before our interview, I attended a lunch at the Jewish Community Center on St. Charles Avenue, where Joan discussed her research on *Quiches, Kugels and Couscous,* while an attentive group feasted on kosher delights. What a wonderful surprise when Mildred Covert herself was the mistress of ceremonies, giving Joan a glowing introduction.

As our *Louisiana Eats!* interview began, Joan stated, "I've always thought there was a big connection between Alsace food and New Orleans food. Bread pudding is much like the original kugel, which is a Sabbath dish. The other thing I noticed is that there are a lot of rouxs in the Alsatian soups, and, of course, you have rouxs here. And when I went to Café du Monde, I noticed that their rectangular donuts are cut exactly like Alsatian donuts are. I realized that these are so old, they're before cookie cutters."

Mildred Covert had made a similar connection. "In Israel," she had told me, "there is something called the *sufganiyot.* It's actually a donut made very similar to the beignets—the basic recipe is very much like the beignets." *Sufganiyot* are usually filled with jelly and eaten during Hanukkah celebrations. So, it seems our classic New Orleans donut has Jewish roots no matter which way you connect it—either through the Jews of Alsace-Lorraine as Joan suggested or through the Israeli tie Mildred spoke of.

In the summer of 2012, I met yet another prominent Jewish figure, Michael Twitty, who was traveling to New Orleans on a journey of self-discovery, something he referred to as the "Southern Discomfort Tour."

Michael is an African-American writer, culinary historian, and historical interpreter, dedicated to preserving and promoting African-American foodways, always with an eye on authentic African origins. He grew up in a nominally Christian household and told his mother at the age of seven that he wanted to be Jewish. Michael credits this early interest to Kemp Mill, the predominantly Orthodox Jewish DC neighborhood in which he grew up. His plan dissolved once his mother explained a certain surgical operation would be necessary for Michael to become a part of the Jewish community.

When he was in college, he once again began to feel the strong pull towards Judaism. Michael studied the religion so that it began to become a part of him in a way that he had never anticipated and could not quite understand.

As his curious explorations continued, a friend gave him an introduction to fellow DC resident Joan Nathan. An initial phone call brought him to her door where, during that very first visit, she taught him how to make challah. When Michael described his intense desire to become Jewish, Joan introduced him to a Sephardic rabbi, who welcomed him into the synagogue where he later formally converted.

"There are Jewish people of color not just in Africa, but in communities all over the world," Michael pointed out to me. "There are black Jews in Cuba. There are black Jews in Brazil. They're in corners of the world you've never thought. When I was researching free families of color in antebellum Charleston, you would not believe how many of them had the last name Cohen or Levi."

Michael is a Judaic Studies high school teacher of mostly Reform Jewish students. His classes include the subject of kosher slaughter. When he broaches this particular subject, he says, "It opens up the classroom to a discussion on ethical eating, on consumption. Do we think about the animals we consume? Do we think about how they are raised? How do we honor the life that's in that food?" Michael says that when his students begin to think about these larger issues, "it just sets the classroom on fire—and that's a good day."

Michael believes that the food he creates is an invitation to understand his complex identity. "If people cannot understand or comprehend me at any other level, they can understand me through my plate." He finished by quoting an ancient African proverb: Sit at my table and you shall know me.

Michael Twitty's Louisiana Latkes

Michael's 2011 travels in the South inspired him to spice up his traditional latke recipe. This is his way of incorporating his newly found Southern identity on the plate.

Yields approximately 1 dozen latkes

2 cups peeled and grated Yukon Gold or Russet potatoes
1 tbsp. grated onion
1 tbsp. chopped celery
2 tbsp. thinly sliced green onion
1 small garlic clove, minced
1 pinch thyme
½ tsp. cayenne pepper
3 eggs, beaten
2 tbsp. all-purpose flour, matzo meal, or potato starch
1½ tsp. salt
½ cup peanut, canola, or vegetable oil
Applesauce, sour cream, or sweet chili sauce, for serving, if desired

Wring the potatoes in a cheesecloth to extract as much moisture as you can; repeat this several times.

In a medium bowl, combine the potato, onion, celery, green onion, garlic, thyme, cayenne pepper, eggs, flour, and salt.

In a large, heavy-bottomed skillet over medium-high heat, heat the oil until hot, usually between 350 and 375 degrees. Place a heaping 1½ tbsp. of the potato mixture into the hot oil, flattening it down to form ¼"- to ½"-thick patties. Brown on one side, turn, and brown on the other. Let drain on paper towels. Serve hot with an extra dusting of cayenne pepper, a few slices of green onion, and any sauces, if desired.

Mildred Covert's Fried Green Tomatoes with Gefilte Fish

A thoroughly Southern dish done Kosher-style!

Yields 4 servings

1 16-oz. jar gefilte fish
2 cups matzo meal
Oil for frying

1 egg
1 cup milk
8 slices green tomato, ¼" thick

Drain the gefilte fish. Roll in matzo meal and fry in oil until lightly browned; set aside.

Mix together the egg and milk to make an egg wash. Dip each slice of green tomato in the egg wash and coat thoroughly with matzo meal. Pan-fry the tomato slices, turning once, until lightly browned on each side.

Top each slice of fried green tomato with several pieces of gefilte fish and lightly drizzle with remoulade sauce. The fried gefilte fish can also be served skewered with toothpicks and passed with kosher remoulade sauce as an appetizer.

Mildred Covert's Kosher Remoulade Sauce

Yields 2 cups

4 tbsp. prepared horseradish
½ cup vinegar
2 tbsp. ketchup
1 tbsp. paprika
½ tsp. cayenne pepper

1 tsp. salt
1 clove garlic
1 cup vegetable oil
½ cup green onions, chopped
½ cup celery, chopped

Combine all ingredients in a blender or food processor and blend thoroughly until smooth. Chill before serving.

Note: if preparing this dish for Passover, make sure that the horseradish, vinegar, and ketchup are labeled "Kosher for Passover."

Joan Nathan's Beignets de Carnaval

Joan was so insistent on the Alsatian-New Orleans connection that we agree that her Beignets de Carnaval are a well-merited addition to this collection. Joan suggests them as a dish for the Jewish holiday Purim, but, as they're fried in oil, they'd be ideal for Hanukkah as well.

Yields 2 dozen

1½ tbsp. active dry yeast
½ cup warm water
4 cups all-purpose flour
3 large eggs
½ tsp. salt

¼ cup granulated sugar
7 tbsp. unsalted butter or margarine, at room temperature
Vegetable oil for frying
Confectioners' sugar

Dissolve the yeast in the water in the bowl of an electric mixer fitted with the dough hook.

Stir in the flour, eggs, salt, granulated sugar, and butter, and knead until you have the consistency of a smooth dough. Turn it out, clean and grease the bowl, and put the dough back in. Allow dough to rest, covered, for 1½ to 2 hours, or until doubled in volume. Punch down, and knead again.

Roll out the dough with a rolling pin to a thickness of about ¼". With a sharp knife, cut the dough into roughly equal 2" triangles or rectangles. Allow to rise for 45 minutes.

Heat about 2" of oil to 375 degrees in a deep pan or a wok. Lower 3 or 4 pieces of the dough at a time into the hot oil, and fry until they are golden on both sides. Extract them with a slotted spoon and drain on paper towels. Repeat with the rest of the dough. Sprinkle with confectioners' sugar before serving. Serve hot!

From Quiches, Kugels, and Couscous: My Search for Jewish Cooking in France *by Joan Nathan, copyright © 2010 by Joan Nathan. Used by permission of Alfred A. Knopf, a division of Random House, Inc.*

PS—I Love the Boys in the Band

When you're married to a man with more than seventy cousins, you're related to the world. Consequently, it should have been no surprise that David Pomerleau, the bass player with the band Johnny Sketch and the Dirty Notes, turned out to be my husband's second cousin as well as a *Louisiana Eats!* fan.

David was traveling to Houston for Thanksgiving with his mom, my husband, Nicky's, cousin Margaret, when the topic of *Louisiana Eats!* came up. It turned out that everyone in the Pomerleau family had become regular listeners of the show. On the drive, David mused that I might be interested in some original music for the show from Johnny Sketch and the band.

At that time, barely six months into the radio show, I was already considering the difference that distinctive, original theme music might do for the sound identification of *Louisiana Eats!*. I hadn't been able to find the exact sound I wanted or the right people to help musically brand the show, but I wanted the opening notes to clearly herald *Louisiana Eats!*.

I saw David at the annual Christmas party, the one occasion that brings together Nicky's many aunts, uncles, cousins, and their offspring. I've been attending this gargantuan affair for more than a quarter-century and must confess that I am still grateful they hand nametags out at the door.

I was already familiar with the Johnny Sketch sound. David, Marc Paradis, and André Bohren had crafted a distinctive, original style in the decade that the band had been together. The three met while studying music at Loyola University. There, they all received training as classical musicians. An intense, New Orleans vibe backs their classical music training, creating a complex but funky sound. Brass player Omar Ramirez became a band member after Hurricane Katrina, adding another layer to the mix.

Marc (Johnny Sketch) primarily plays lead guitar, but the real showpiece instrument in the band is his electric cello. David contributes a heavy line of funk on bass guitar, and André keeps the beat on drums. Marc and David's harmonizing vocals knit a fabric of sound tighter and tighter.

When David offered to write some original music for *Louisiana Eats!*, I immediately knew it would be a perfect fit. David went to work on what was to become his first solo musical composition recorded by the band. "Usually, Marc has an idea and brings it to Dré and me and we all work it out collaboratively," he told me.

WWNO station manager Paul Maassen negotiated a professional trade in kind with Mark Bingham of Piety Street Recording for studio time, and in early 2011 we all met there to lay down the track.

I agreed to credit the original theme music to Johnny Sketch and the Dirty Notes at the close of each week's episode. And for lagniappe, I showed up at the recording session with Central Grocery muffulettas and drinks to fuel the band. I also promised to cook a celebratory dinner for the band so that we could listen to the official *Louisiana Eats!* theme music debut together. David's original music, as performed by Johnny Sketch, had just the funky, down-and-dirty sound that I wanted for *Louisiana Eats!* On February 9, 2011, in an episode entitled "Love At First Bite," Johnny Sketch and the Dirty Notes began opening and closing each episode of the show.

In the spring of 2012, when Lynne Rossetto Kasper and Sally Swift of NPR's *Splendid Table* traveled to New Orleans with *Road Food* hosts Jane and Michael Stern, WWNO hosted a live taping of *Louisiana Eats!*. The event was held in the Grand Ballroom of the Royal Sonesta Hotel, and Johnny and the boys functioned as our house band, adding just the perfect edge of coolness to the evening.

That summer, I got an emergency text message from Marc, aka Johnny Sketch. The band was performing on the road in Destin, Florida. He wrote, "Poppy, we've got all these donuts and we want to make bread pudding. What should we do?" I sent Marc instructions as to how best to transform the donuts into authentic, New Orleans bread pudding, and at the same time I made a mental note of what a fun interview the mash-up of musicians and the food that fuels them could be.

I'd already done some thinking along those lines. My friend Anne Churchill, the chef/owner of Karma Kitchen catering, had traveled as road chef with the Dave Matthews Band. I had long wanted to get Anne to tell some road stories on *Louisiana Eats!*.

It all came together in the spring of 2013 and made for a perfect Jazz Fest *Louisiana Eats!* episode. The Dave Matthews Band was scheduled to perform at the fest, and Johnny Sketch and the Dirty Notes were playing a headlining act at Acura Stage, debuting their first new CD in five years. I knew that the dichotomy of road food in the big leagues—the Dave Matthews Band entourage travels in an eleven-bus caravan—as compared to Johnny Sketch's modest road-food experiences would border on the absurd and make for really good content.

Anne Churchill and I often see each other in passing at the Crescent City Farmers Market. Even when just shopping at the market, Anne often has a rock star vibe of her own. When Anne arrived at the studio for her interview, I was immediately captivated by a necklace of carved jade on an intricate silver chain that resembled a Buddha's Hand citrus.

I began the interview by asking Anne the back story of her relationship with the Dave Matthews Band. "I'd had a working relationship with Piety Street Studios previously," she said. "They had hired me to cook for Elvis Costello and Allen Toussaint when they recorded *River in Reverse* there. It was pretty exciting getting to feed them!"

"Then, I was at a Christmas party in the Bywater and Sean Hall of Piety Street Studios told me, 'We might have a band coming in that might need a caterer, but we can't tell you who it is yet. They might want to bring in their own chef, but I told them I thought they just might want you to cook for them.'"

Anne discovered who the mysterious entity was when she got a phone call from Cara of the Dave Matthews Band management asking for some sample menus. Anne learned they were coming to New Orleans to record the CD that became *Big Whiskey and GrooGrux King.* This was a short time after Hurricane Katrina and just after one of their band members, LeRoi Moore, had passed away. LeRoi had loved the city, so the band thought it would be a great tribute to him if they recorded the new CD here, simultaneously contributing to the rebuilding of New Orleans.

The band reviewed Anne's menus. "They realized, 'Oh, she gets it. She can do the kind of food we want,'" Anne said. She got the job and was responsible for cooking three meals per day for the many months the band lived in New Orleans.

"It was challenging to come up with so many different menus. They loved my meat-stuffed mushrooms, which are like a meatball over a portabella mushroom, topped with a sauce. Dave freaked out over that," Anne remembered. "I did a lot of Southeast Asian stuff and also bought a half of a Pineywoods cattle steer from heritage-breed cattle rancher Justin Pitts, so they ate a lot of local, grass-fed beef."

As the CD was about to wrap, "I was setting up for dinner one night and someone mentioned a tour chef,"

she recalled. Anne wasn't aware that a job like that existed, but when she learned that tour chefs travel with the band and cook for them on the road, she exclaimed, "Are you kidding me? That's a job?" Seeing her enthusiasm, "They asked if I'd be interested. I was newly single and thought, 'I can pick up and take off for months at a time—sure!' That's how I started working for their catering team," Anne said.

She became part of the road team that consists of "four chefs, a front-of-house dining-room person, a crew chief, and someone who handles stocking the dressing rooms and the buses." Her first trip out with the band was a summer tour, all in outdoor amphitheaters. "In the band's rider that is advanced to the venue, it states that they have to provide a tent of certain dimensions," Anne related. "They have to provide us with refrigeration, tables, and a few prep cook/dishwasher people—although on bad days, we have to jump in and wash dishes too."

When the caravan arrives at a destination, "breakfast is usually pre-shopped, but the lead chef immediately goes out to a store and buys the lunch and dinner food while the remaining three of us set up. The road cases come off the truck with convection ovens, pots, pans, an entire pantry, a whole front-of-house with chafing dishes, and a giant coffee case," Anne said. The equipment for catering alone takes an entire bus to transport.

When the kitchen space is organized they immediately would "crank out breakfast for about eighty-five people. Fiona, the lead chef, returns and we unload and talk about lunch. Then we crank out lunch. As soon as it's out, we talk about dinner and keep lunch going while we get dinner ready for five o'clock. Dinner goes till eight or eight-thirty each night; then we pack everything up, get on the bus, and go to another town and do it again."

Life as a tour chef could be harrowing, Anne recalled. "There was one weather situation on a summer tour when we arrived during a giant thunder and lightning storm. Water was getting in our cases and the wind was blowing things over, so we couldn't set up and had to wing it. I found a little alcove inside and put out breakfast while the guys outside wrestled with flying tarps. It's really the same as with catering and working in restaurants. You think you're not going to pull it off and all of a sudden then, you think, 'I just can't believe I pulled that off again!'"

I had heard crazy stories about demands that bands made in their riders (backstage specifications) and asked Anne about that. "That really came about when the first big rock concerts were being done indoors," she said. "The stakes are high, considering how dangerous the set-ups can be with equipment and electricity. So, the band's tour manager would send out these riders with strange stipulations like, 'No red M&M's; only brown M&M's are allowed backstage.' The venue management was supposed to read and follow these riders to a T. Often, the odd stipulations were hidden at the end of the rider. So, if the M&M's weren't the right colors, it proved to the tour manager the promoter hadn't read the document to the end. It wasn't that the rock bands were prima donnas," she explained.

"I know people think it's just a wild party all the time, but it's an intense job where you worked hard every day. But, occasionally there'll be a bus party with lots of music, dancing, and . . ." Anne's voice trailed off in laughter. "It's an intense job. It's hard on the body and it can be a little hard on the liver. You're in close confines with a lot of people. You're living on a bus with seven other people and you work with them for fifteen hours a day, then you're hanging out with them at night. Sometimes, you just want to go be by yourself for a little while."

The Johnny Sketch road-food scene is quite different from Anne's Dave Matthews experience. For the Johnny Sketch interview, three band members had agreed to meet me on a Tuesday at the WWNO studio: drummer André Bohren, bass player (and cousin) David Pomerleau, and guitarist and cellist Marc Paradis. Arriving at the station, I found only Marc waiting. "Where are the rest of the guys?" I asked. Marc answered, "David can't make it and Dré is on the way." David had apparently gotten his dates and times confused and had begged-off with Marc on the phone just minutes before.

This was not going to work for me or for them. For the interview to have the maximum impact, we needed more voices and more conversation to create the full two-part interview I had envisioned. So, I called David myself.

"How long will it take you to get here?" I asked him. "I'm so sorry, Poppy. I spaced it out . . ." he answered. "But when can you be here, David?" I asked again. When he tried to refuse a second time, I pulled out the stops and threatened, "Don't make me call your grandmother!" referring to my husband's Aunt Blanche, David's "Granny." Blanche Comisky, mother of eleven children and grandmother and great-grandmother to more than forty, ruled the roost with an iron hand and was not one to mess with. That did the trick, and David promised he was on the way.

As we did studio sound checks, I asked Marc what they'd named the new CD. "I'm not sure," he answered. "Marc," I replied, "We have to call the new CD by name in this interview if you want to actually promote it!"

"Well," Marc said, "The name I like is *Two Thousand Days*. That's how long it's been since our last CD was released, and look—here's the artwork for the cover." Marc passed me his iPhone with the image of the CD cover on the screen. On a mustard-colored background, an intricate line-drawing of an East Indian elephant appeared, complete with an ornate seat on its back as if awaiting a rider.

"That's perfect!" I told him. As André walked into the studio, I asked, "André, what's the name of the new CD?" "*Two Thousand Days,*" he answered. Then David walked in and I asked him the same question and got the same answer. "So that's it! *Two Thousand Days* it is!" I exclaimed, and the new CD got its name.

We began by talking about the process of recording *Two Thousand Days*. Marc said, "We recorded at the Music Shed at Euterpe and Annunciation Street." André added, "In December, we were in there for a full week; then, in January, we had another couple of days."

Their average recording session lasted ten hours, but they agreed that this was the most efficient record the band had ever made. After all, as the title suggested, "We had two thousand days to prepare for it. We've been performing a lot of these songs, in some cases, for years, so we knew what we had to do when we got in there. It sounds really good because we were ready," David pointed out.

"We've been together for eleven and a half years. Tracey Freeman mixed the new CD, and he is the one really responsible for making it sound so good. He is a big step up for us as far as working with really talented producers. What he did with the tracks was remarkable. He's done Kermit Ruffins. He's Harry Connick Jr.'s producer. He has three Grammys."

"He's about to have four of them when this comes out!" Marc warned. "That's right—The fourth Grammy is coming up, Freeman."

Tracey Freeman's influence also extended to what the band ate while recording at Music Shed Studios. He'd not only mixed the music but provided catering as well. "Tracey Freeman had the genius idea to stop at Dorignac's every day on the way to the studio and buy three poor boy loaves, Chisesi Ham, all the good in-house cured meats from the deli counter, sliced Swiss, tomatoes, lettuce . . . It was a great way to take a break," Marc reminisced. "You go in and build yourself a sandwich. I'm a big sandwich fan. They call me Captain Sandwich, so I was in heaven. Every day, making up sandwiches with egg salad, tuna salad . . . The poor boy thing was absolutely genius and I would recommend it to anyone making a record. It was great, and, actually, it was pretty cost-effective too!"

The boys in the band are well-accustomed to trying to control food costs. André spoke fondly of their old van, the one they'd called "Murph." "Our old van treated us very well for many years. We used to do a lot more groceries on the road rather than just eating at restaurants. I used to make the sandwiches in the front seat and pass them back, so I got to know everyone's preference. No mayonnaise for Nick, no tomatoes for David, and everything for Marc. We called it the 'Murph Special.' It was a just a cheese sandwich, but we'd put tomatoes, cucumbers, hummus, and sprouts, lots of veggies. It's a great sandwich."

After more than eleven years together on the road, the band has regular stops they never miss. André is so enthusiastic about road food that he claims, "I've said for years that 40 percent of the reason I want to be in a touring band is to sample the world's biscuits and gravy. I'm on a constant quest. And now, I'm not the only one. We even named a song 'Biscuits and Gravy.' Those are the only words in that song."

When in Destin, Florida, the band never misses a stop at the Donut Hole. That's how the bread pudding dilemma arose. Marc told me, "It was three o'clock in the morning after the gig and the woman was throwing away these giant bags of donuts." David continued, "So, I just had to ask her, 'Are you throwing those out? Because we'll take them.' She gave us like, two hundred donuts. We ate a couple, but we had to do something with them. The bread pudding turned out amazing, incredible! It was all about the sauce for me—it's the whiskey."

They recalled a greasy spoon in North Carolina where the cooking was done out back on a tiny grill. Everyone chimed in with food memories from the Abbey in Baltimore, where they make burgers from crocodile, kangaroo, elk, ostrich, and bison. They described it as "a tiny place on Federal Hill Alley, near a club where we usually play, 'The Eight by Ten.'"

David said, "The best Philly cheesesteak I've ever had was not in Philadelphia. It was in Key West, Florida, at Mr. Z's, but the guys who run the place are from Philadelphia."

"We've probably spent half the money we've made in Key West at Mr. Z's," Marc mused. "It's a quarter of a block from where we play, and it's open 'til five in the morning. They're always grumpy, but just enough."

After hearing Anne's story about the rider, I asked about their rider. Marc laughed and said, "Yeah, we've heard of those. We say that we need water."

"And a case of beer and towels," David added, "And we don't even specify what kind of beer."

"You wouldn't believe how many places where we show up, and there's twenty little cups of water on the stage and that's our allowance," Marc complained. "We're not Journey or anything, but we can't get a case of water? A whole bottle of water for just myself? Then what happens is David and I are sharing one, and it gets real awkward."

On the positive side, David noted, "But, at a lot of the festivals, we have had some amazing hospitality. The Telluride Blues and Brews Festival is as close to the big time that we've made. They were so cool with the artists. It didn't matter if you were the Black Crows or us. We got massages, food, and unlimited micro-brewed beer. And, on Sunday morning, everybody got their own bottle of champagne for mimosas."

"Some venues are very professional," David continued. "Like the Belly Up in Aspen. For the pre-show meal, they sat us down and put out big serving dishes. It was the employee meal, but it was really great eating. We see the opposite so much that the fact we even remember eating at the Belly Up—and that was in 2007—really says something."

"We knew we had made it when we played at Tipitina's and they had Popeye's waiting for us," Marc interjected. "If you go backstage and they have the twenty-piece mixed and some sides, you feel like a rock star. And at Jazz Fest, Quint has always been so supportive. He introduces us, and we love the little wedge sandwiches they always have for us backstage."

As we ended the interview, I thanked them again for the *Louisiana Eats!* theme music and André said, "Do you know what we named that song?" This was the first I'd ever heard that the song had a name. "That song is called, 'Let's Eat,' which was almost the name of our first record," Marc answered. "We've been trying to call something 'Let's Eat' forever."

That's why I love the boys in the band.

Crawfish Étouffeé

My dear friend, New Orleans cooking teacher Lee Barnes, shared this étouffée recipe with me many years ago. Lee said she'd learned it from an old man who mostly spoke Cajun French. By watching and tasting what he did, she learned how to cook it. This recipe is so easy and quick—it's ready before the rice is finished! You can make it with shrimp, too. It's so richly buttery and delicious that I knew that Johnny and the boys would love it. This is what I served the night of my special "thank you" dinner.

Yields 4 servings

½ cup butter
3 tbsp. tomato paste
6-8 green onions, thinly sliced
1 tsp. thyme
2 bay leaves
½ tsp. salt

1 tsp. freshly ground black pepper
1 tbsp. hot sauce
1 lb. crawfish tails
1 cup water
1 clove garlic, minced
Cooked rice, for serving

Melt butter and whisk in tomato paste. Add the green onions, herbs, salt, pepper, and hot sauce. Cook together for 5 minutes.

Rinse out the crawfish-tail bag with water to gather remaining fat and whisk liquid into the butter mixture. Add the garlic and the crawfish tails. Cover and cook over low heat for about 5 minutes. Serve over rice.

Stuffed Portabella Mushrooms

Anne Churchill generously shared her recipe for the stuffed portabella mushrooms that were such a hit with the Dave Matthews Band.

Yields 6 servings

6 4-5"-wide portabella mushrooms, wiped clean of any dirt
¼ cup olive oil
2 tbsp. butter
1 medium onion, chopped
3 garlic cloves, minced
1 lb. ground beef

1 lb. ground pork
1 cup cooked brown rice
1 tbsp. flat-leaf parsley, chopped
3 tbsp. chili garlic sauce
1 tbsp. Lea & Perrins Worcestershire sauce
2 tbsp. Creole mustard
½ tsp. salt

Preheat oven to 350 degrees.

Finely chop the stems of the portabella mushrooms, reserving the caps. Using a spoon, gently scrape the gills from the inside of each mushroom. Place the mushrooms, top-side up, on a 17" baking pan. Pour the olive oil into the pan and turn the mushrooms once to coat both sides.

Melt the butter in a skillet. Add the onion, garlic and chopped mushroom stems. Sauté until the onion is translucent. Remove from heat and cool to room temperature.

In a bowl, combine the sautéed vegetables with the ground beef, ground pork, rice, parsley, chili garlic sauce, Worcestershire sauce, Creole mustard, and salt. Form 6 large patties and mold them into the cavity of each Portabella mushroom.

Place the stuffed mushrooms in a roasting pan and cover with aluminum foil. Bake for 25 minutes. Remove the foil and continue baking for another 15 minutes or until nicely browned. Spoon pan gray over mushrooms. Serve hot.

Donut Bread Pudding

Here's the recipe I sent Marc to solve the Destin-donut dilemma.

Serves at least 8 hungry band members

8 eggs
1½ cups milk
½ cup sugar, optional
1 tsp. vanilla extract

4 dozen donut holes
½ cup butter, room temperature
1 cup powdered sugar
½ cup bourbon, or to taste

Preheat oven to 350 degrees.

Mix together the eggs, milk, sugar, and vanilla. Add the donut holes, breaking them up with your hands as you add them to the liquid. If the donuts were stale and you can't squeeze milk out of the mixture once they are combined, add a bit more milk.

Pour the pudding into a greased, 13" x 9" baking pan and bake for approximately 45 minutes, until the pudding is lightly browned on top.

In a medium bowl, beat the butter and powdered sugar together until smooth. Beat in the bourbon. Spread the butter sauce over the hot bread pudding and serve.

Acknowledgments

Without the *Louisiana Eats!* radio show, this book might never have been written. I owe a tremendous amount of gratitude to my sound engineer and co-producer, Thomas Walsh, who helped make sure that I had all the audio needed to construct the book. From the show's earliest days, Thomas has been a valued partner in both the show's construction and its evolution.

Diana Pinckley, Ron Biava, and WWNO station manager Paul Maassen's brainstorm, as later named by Pinckley's husband, John Pope, were all essential ingredients in the early mix. They believed that food radio was what the WWNO listeners were hungry for. *Louisiana Eats!* braved the way for a major change from all-day classical music to talk and news programming with an emphasis on locally produced shows.

Without really knowing what the final product would be, Brian and Leslie Burkey of the Wine Institute of New Orleans, Michael Morse of Zatarain's, restaurateur Dickie Brennan, the Whann family of Leidenheimer Baking Company, and my beloved next door neighbors, Jennifer and Charlie Eagan of Leitz-Eagan Funeral Home, all bravely stepped up to the plate and sponsored our first year. Thank you all for your confidence in me.

Thanks to all of the wonderful people who have shared their stories with us on *Louisiana Eats!*. Whether by phone, in person at the studio, or out on the field (and sometimes even literally), the conversations have been a special treat that I hope will provide value as oral histories about our culture and heritage.

My editor and dear friend Sara Roahen helped me craft the written word that is this book. Without Sara's smart suggestions, her ability to speak to me in my own words, and her deep and intimate knowledge of both the subjects and subject matter, this book would simply not be the final product you hold in your hands today. I couldn't have done it without you, Sara—really!

From the time I first became acquainted with David Spielman's style of portraiture, I knew the difference that David's portrayals of my *Louisiana Eats!* subject matter would bring to this book. Thank you, David, for bringing my vision to these pages.

I also offer a special thanks to photographer David Gallant, whose portrait of Mildred Covert helped save the day when, unfortunately, Mildred was in transition and unable to sit for David.

My master indexing, formatting, and just plain patient and helpful husband, Nicky, was instrumental in producing the professional document that became the final version of this book. Thank you, Nicky, and thanks to all of my friends and family who understood the months of work that kept me away from fun. Now, let's make up for it!

In fact, in the words of Johnny Sketch and the Dirty Notes, "Let's eat!"

Index